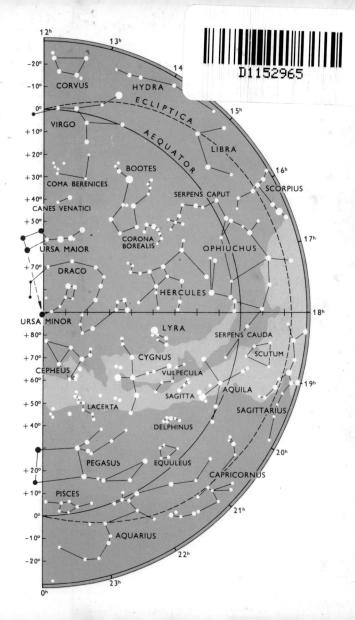

CONSTELLATIONS

a concise guide in colour

CONSTELLATIONS

by Josef Klepešta
and Antonín Rükl

HAMLYN
London • New York • Sydney • Toronto

Cover photograph of the Trifid Nebular in Sagittarius, M. 20 is
by courtesy of Mt. Wilson and Palomar Observatories and
California Institute of Technology

Translated by Olga Kuthanová
Designed and produced by ARTIA for
THE HAMLYN PUBLISHING GROUP LTD
LONDON · NEW YORK · SYDNEY · TORONTO
Astronaut House, Feltham, Middlesex, England
© Copyright 1969 by Artia
Reprinted 1972, 1974, 1975

ISBN 0 600 00893 2

Printed in Czechoslovakia
3/02/09/51

Contents

The Stellar ABC

In this day and age when journeys into interplanetary space are a common subject of discussion man is showing an increasing interest in the stars as beacons for putting space probes into orbit. When such a journey takes place, one reads in the pages of the daily and scientific press the strange and fascinating names of the stars and constellations in the heavens. When Mariner 4 was launched, an orientating manoeuvre was made after 16 hours of flight in geocentric orbit. First of all the probe's sensor located the star Markab in the constellation Pegasus and shortly afterwards the bright star Aldebaran in Taurus. As neither of these stars had been chosen for navigation of the probe in interplanetary space, Mariner 4 received orders to locate the star Canopus in Carina in the southern sky. This it succeeded in doing and it subsequently safely reached its destination — the planet Mars.

Origin of Stellar Nomenclature

A striking feature of the space age is the use of ancient names for stars and constellations in connection with the latest technical developments. The names of the stars date from the time when the natural sciences flourished in Arabia and Persia, among them *astrognosis* — or knowledge of the stars. On the other hand, the names of the constellations are, with a few exceptions, of Greek and Roman origin.

It is unlikely that we shall ever find unequivocal evidence as to when names were first given to certain groups of stars. The first to be conceived, most probably, were the symbols for the Sun, Moon and planets, because their real and imaginary influence on the life of primitive man was the most marked. Individual stars and groups of stars acquired their names by chance and without pattern. The stars were of interest to sailors for ascertaining the position of the ship. The rising and setting of certain stars marked the beginning of a stormy season at sea or a season that was favourable for sailing. In the same way farmers and shepherds could tell by the stars when was the best time for sowing and reaping. As there were no written records, this information was generally preserved as tradition, based on past experience and handed down from generation to generation.

The first records of the names of small groups of stars centred on brighter stars come from Mesopotamia. Texts preserved on clay tablets bear such names as 'king star', 'stormy bird', 'dog of the sungod', etc.

In the third century BC, Aratos of Soli, physician and poet at the court of the Macedonian king Antigonos Gonatas, did much towards unifying the various constellations and their names. Prominent star groups were given names related to Greek mythology and all this he wrote down on a roll of manuscript entitled *Phainomena*, of which only fragments have been preserved. One copy, dating from the ninth to tenth century AD, was supplemented by Father Geruvius with a star map depicting all the symbols listed by Aratos in his manuscript. This classification survived many centuries, during which there were many attempts to change what were considered as pagan conceptions. The *Phainomena* of Aratos served as an inspiration for several poetic works. One of the best is *Fasti*, a calendar by the Roman poet Publius Ovidius Naso (Ovid). *Fasti* was a paean to life, describing the Roman feasts and their origins. At many points the

10

poet refers to the rising and setting of certain stars, thus testifying to man's interest in the stars at that time.

Ovid's poem also bears evidence of the author's interest in the stars, namely his knowledge of the variable brightness of one of the stars in the Pleiades which we know today is enveloped in a shroud of nebulae. Modern science can explain this natural phenomenon with the help of a wide range of powerful and complicated instruments. But it is most remarkable that the poet should have noted this fact with the unaided eye almost two thousand years ago. Ovid wrote:

Scorpium in coelo, quum cras lucescere Nonas
*Dicimus a media parte videndus erit.**

Scorpius will be seen in the middle part of the sky
when we say that tomorrow the Nones will begin to shine.

Virgil was another Roman poet who took an interest in the stars. The son of a farmer, he put much of his knowledge into writing in his *Georgics*, which fully deserves to be considered as a book of advice to farmers, for it urges them to learn about the stars whose rising and setting tell when and what work should be done if a successful outcome be desired. Speaking of bees, he tells what time is best for collecting the honey:

Bis gravidos cogunt fetus, duo tempora messis,
Taygete simul os terris ostendit honestum
Plias et Oceani spretos pede reppulit amnis,
Aut eadem sidus fugiens ubi Piscis aqueosi
*Tristior hibernas coelo descendit in undas.***

---

* Ovid, *Fasti*, Book V (May), verse 417 and 418.
** Virgil, *Georgics*, Book IV, Episode I, On collecting honey.

*Twice do they [the bee-keepers] gather in the honey
yield, there are two seasons of harvest so; soon
as the Pleiad Taygete has shown to Earth her comely
face, and spurned and dashed beneath her foot the
Ocean river; or when the same star, as she flies
from the constellation of the rainy Fish [Pisces],
more sorrowfully descends from heaven into the
winter-waves.*

Every culture had its own conception of the stars.
The European, influenced by the ancient Greeks and
Romans, differed from the Asiatic conception, and
that in turn differed from what the records and
monuments of the original inhabitants of the South
American continent tell us. The Arabic culture left
a permanent imprint on the naming of stars. This came
about in the first millenium AD when Islamic learning
flourished on the Arabian peninsula and in Persia. In
those days scholars in the service of the great caliphs
observed the heavens for the purposes of astrology
and science.

The Arabs and Persians adopted many myths about
the skies from the Greeks and Romans, sometimes
giving them a unique flavour of their own. They
described the Milky Way as a great river, stretching
across the heavens, alongside which grazed slim-legged
gazelles, ostriches, camels and thorough-bred stallions.
The tents were surrounded by oases with date palms,
and in the centre of this promised land of Allah lay
a treasure chest full of glittering jewels. Of this beautiful fantasy which inspired poets to glowing phrases,
nothing remains but the names of a few stars and the
glittering treasure chest — the star cluster near the
star $\varkappa$ Crucis.

The names Sirius and Procyon are of ancient origin

as well. It is known that their heliacal rising was eagerly awaited in the Nile delta, for that was a sure sign of the onset of the rainy season.

All the various epochs have left records of astronomical interest on the observation of new stars and the circumstances illustrating the origin of their names. Sometimes these data were hewn in rock; at other times they were written on papyrus or parchment. One of the strangest histories is connected with the record made in Chinese annals by an unknown astronomer at the court of the famous Sung dynasty. At that time it was the duty of the astronomers to watch the skies and to inform the emperor the instant anything unusual appeared — say a meteor, comet or new star. One such event is recorded in the annals as follows.

'In the first year of the Chi-ho era [i.e. in the year 1054 AD] in the fifth month of Chih'-cou [July 4], there appeared in the sky a visiting star near the star T'ien-kuan [ζ Tauri]. After somewhat more than a year it was no longer visible.' Another report states that 'the star was visible in the daytime for twenty-three days and rays spurted from it on all sides. Its light was a pinkish colour.'

The mysterious star disappeared from the sky and from people's memory. Centuries passed and one generation followed another, until in the eighteenth century the French astronomer Charles Messier compiled a list of nebulae, the first of which was the small cloud near ζ Tauri. Another century passed before Lord Rosse of Parsonstown with his huge reflector resolved the strange arms of the nebula, the whole bearing a vague resemblance to a crab; and Crab Nebula is the name it goes by to this day. The greatest surprise came, however, when photographs were made of this nebula and its spectrum was ascertained. The

13

study of this spectrum revealed that a vast nuclear process is taking place in the heart of the nebula. The nucleus is a gigantic cyclotron whose diameter is continuously expanding. It was evident to astronomers that this was a classic example of a supernova. They deduced from the rate of expansion of the nebula's diameter that the supernova must have exploded some 800—900 years ago. Professor J. L. Duyvendak found the above-mentioned records in the ancient Chinese annals, and these have furnished proof that the Crab Nebula is nothing more than the remnants of a still active supernova observed in 1054 by an unknown Chinese astronomer at the imperial court.

What Light Has to Tell Us

For thousands of years men gazed at the stars without the slightest hope of ever learning the truth about the energy that has kept them burning so long. Only a hundred years ago it would still have been difficult to describe the nature of any individual star. However, modern instruments enable astrophysicists to analyze a star's light and thus to learn of the processes taking place in the interior as well as on the surface of the star. Today we know that each star is a sun, or rather an atomic reactor, in its own right. What role does light play in this connection?

The dictionary tells us that light is an electromagnetic radiation which travels from a star into space in all directions. We know that electromagnetic radiations range in wavelength from gamma-rays through X-rays, ultraviolet, visible and infrared light to radio waves, and all these radiations are governed by the same laws, for basically they are of the same kind, differing only in wavelength. What is it that makes up a wave of electromagnetic radiation? According to the quantum theory of the German physicist Max Planck, radiation is emitted not in a continuous flow but in the form of separate packets, each composed of a number of small, indivisible units of energy called quanta. Light quanta, or photons, have various energies depending on their frequency. A glowing body such as a star shoots off photons which travel at the speed of light (186,000 miles per second) bearing with them information about their creation. We do not know what happens after the instant a photon leaves a star at the speed of light. It may retain this speed for millions of years; in an optically denser medium it travels more slowly, but on leaving the medium it immediately regains its original speed, which remains constant for any length of time, for in a vacuum it can travel neither slower nor faster.

Because of the great distances between the source of light and the Earth, what we see in the heavens is not what exists there today. The nearest star is viewed by the terrestrial observer as it was four years ago. If Proxima Centauri were suddenly to become cold and inert, we would continue to see it for another four years before knowing that anything had happened, for its light takes exactly four years to reach the Earth. The other stars appear to us as they were even longer ago, hundreds and even thousands of years. If all the stars were suddenly to become cold and inert, man would admire their splendour for centuries more, even though they no longer actually existed. Thus stellar astronomy has become a science concerned with phenomena long since past.

A different problem is posed by the great number of stars. Are they permanent or transient? Are they large or small? Our Sun may be said to be a dwarf star, for there are others far greater and brighter. The number of stars, usually grouped in galaxies, is enormous. Our Galaxy, the Milky Way, alone has about a hundred thousand million. These stars are spaced far apart, the estimated diameter of the Milky Way being 100,000 light years. The Earth and our Sun are located at about the midpoint of one of its radii. As the Earth lies inside the Milky Way, we see the combined light of its many stars as a hazy, silvery band passing through the numerous constellations of the summer and winter nights. It appears to be motionless in the heavens. In reality, however, it revolves around its own centre once in 220 million years.

Newton's Discovery

Like most great discoveries this one had very simple beginnings. In 1666 Isaac Newton bought a glass prism 'to try therewith the celebrated phenomena of colours'. The coloured band formed by the decomposition of white light Newton called the 'spectrum'. He believed he was on the trail of one of nature's great secrets and in 1672 submitted an account entitled 'New Theory of Light and Colours' to the Royal Society, pointing out that this was probably the greatest discovery ever made. Newton's opinion was no exaggeration; he had no inkling, however, how important it was to prove in the future. The natural philosophers of his day considered his idea fantastic. He became subject to criticism which did not cease even after his death. As late as 1790 the famous German poet Goethe proclaimed that the idea of white light being composed of colours was absurd and a tale fit only for children.

The cries of doubt, however, lessened when the renowned German optician Joseph Fraunhofer discovered in 1818 that the coloured band of the Sun's spectrum also contains unusual dark lines whose position remains constant. Later laboratory experiments showed that the Fraunhofer lines (as they are called) are produced by absorption when the source of a continuous spectrum is viewed through the cooler gases of those elements providing the continuous spectrum (in the case of the Sun, the photosphere and the reversing layer above it). A bright line spectrum is provided by the Sun's chromosphere. Fraunhofer and, later, other scientists observed the stars through telescopes equipped with spectroscopes and discovered that the stars have different spectra. They found that the spectra of yellow to red stars contain a great number of the dark lines produced by metals, whereas in the white and blue stars there are fewer of these lines. This was the first, though rough, indication of the significance of stellar spectra; it marked the beginning of man's investigation of the physical composition of the stars. In the mid-nineteenth century Father Angelo Secchi introduced a broader classification along these lines, but it was not until 1874 that the German astronomer H. C. Vogel explained the stellar spectra. The basis of all stellar spectra is the continuous spectrum, which is viewed as a continuous band of varying colours arranged in the following order: violet, blue, green, yellow, orange, red. As in the case of our Sun, the light which forms the continuous spectrum emanates from the star's surface and sub-surface layers. Appearing against this background are the dark absorption lines, which according to Vogel originate in the cooler layer of the star's atmosphere, and last of all the bright emission lines which originate in the hot gaseous shell of the star. This was the first scientific explanation of stellar spectra, though it was far from being fully adequate.

In time, particularly with the introduction of the mass photography of stellar spectra, astrophysicists accumulated extensive information which provided better and more detailed knowledge of the star's physical characteristics. During many decades, Harvard College Observatory in the United States has investigated so many stellar spectra by this method that the result is a catalogue of several volumes containing the spectra of some 225,300 stars. These have been divided into ten principal classes and thirty sub-classes.

It is impossible in a book of this sort to go into the details of spectrum analysis; so the following brief characteristics of stellar spectra will have to suffice. It should be noted at this point that the surface temperatures are given in degrees on the Kelvin scale, which is based not on the freezing point of water (0 °C), as the centigrade scale is, but on absolute zero, which equals −273.16 °C.

Type

Q — spectra typical of novae and supernovae.

W — very hot stars with a temperature of about 50,000 °K.

O — stars with a temperature of about 35,000 °K.

B — the so-called helium stars with a surface temperature of about 20,000 °K.

A — the so-called hydrogen stars whose spectra are characterized by the lines of hydrogen and metals; approximate temperature 10,000 °K.

F — stars whose spectrum is marked by more intense lines of metals; effective temperature between 8000° and 6000 °K.

G — group of stars (which also includes our Sun) whose spectrum has a large number of dark

18

absorption lines; surface temperature approximately 6000 °K.

K — dark absorption lines of metals predominate in the spectrum and bands originating from molecules begin to appear. The surface temperature decreases to 4500 °K.

M — red stars whose spectra are characterized by numerous lines of metals and a preponderance of bands originating from molecules; surface temperature drops to 3500 °K.

RN — the so-called carbon stars; they are cooler stars, and the colour red predominates.

S — a very rare type of spectrum found in relatively cool stars.

Classification according to the type of spectrum has recently been augmented by data relating to the stars' luminosity. In this connection stars are designated as sub-giants, giants and super-giants, as well as sub-dwarfs and dwarfs.

Apparent and Absolute Brightness

One of the first things measured by man was the illumination produced by the Sun's rays. To be able to measure the intensity of light he introduced the unit of illumination called the *lux* and stated that when the Sun is at the zenith the illumination of the Earth's surface is equal to 100,000 lux. This illumination can be produced by 100,000 candles at a distance of one metre. In view of the fact that part of the Sun's light is absorbed, reflected and dispersed by the Earth's atmosphere, the actual intensity of the Sun's light above this atmosphere is 136,000 lux. Quite rightly we may ask how it is possible not to be blinded by this bright light when we can read by the light of a single candle and the illumination of a schoolroom is 100 lux at the most, whilst 100 000 lux is a thousand times as much. The reason is to be found in that remarkable organ, the human eye, which automatically adapts itself to differences in light intensity. If it did not, we would either be blinded by the light in the daytime or unable to see at all at night, as is the case in some animals. It has been determined that if illumination increases in geometrical progression, then its perception by the eye increases in arithmetical progression, which means that the eye does not perceive the real difference in intensity but only its ratio. At low intensities the eye is uncommonly sensitive. There is every reason to believe that the minute energy of a single photon can be perceived as light by the eye. This involves a sort of chain reaction whose mechanism is being studied by modern biology.

Stellar brightness, or *magnitude*, is expressed by Pogson's formula, according to which a star differing from another by one degree of magnitude is two and a half times brighter or fainter than the other. The star Vega in Lyra has a magnitude of 0.1. The greater this number, the fainter the star; e.g. Polaris has a magnitude of 2.2. The naked eye is just able to distinguish stars of the 6th magnitude. Stars brighter than Vega have a negative magnitude; for example, Sirius has a magnitude of −1.6. These magnitudes, however, refer only to the apparent visual brightness of the stars and do not correspond to their actual brightness, which as a rule is quite different. This is caused chiefly by the differences in the stars' distances from the Earth. That is why a star's magnitude is expressed by two different numbers — one denotes its brightness as viewed by the terrestrial observer, and the other, called the *absolute magnitude*, and determined by calcula-

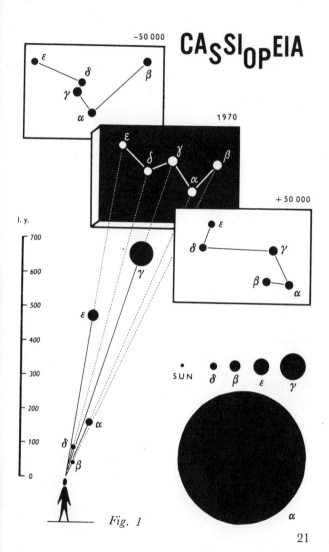

CASSIOPEIA

-50 000

1970

+50 000

l. y.

700

600

500

400

300

200

100

0

SUN δ β ε γ

Fig. 1

21

tions based on the star's apparent magnitude and distance from the Earth, tells us how bright the star would be if it were located at a distance of 10 parsecs (32.6 light years) from the Earth.

This is best illustrated by Fig. 1, which gives three examples showing the motion of the stars in the constellation Cassiopeia, stars which are arranged at the present time in the shape of a W. Our generation and later generations will not perceive this motion, but the picture shows how this constellation appeared 50,000 years ago and how it appears now. It also shows the distance of the individual stars from the Earth in light years. The difference in size of the individual circles indicates the *absolute* magnitude of the stars, thereby enabling comparison with their *apparent* magnitude. Finally, in the bottom right-hand corner there is a comparison of the diameters of the stars in Cassiopeia with that of the Sun. The illustration shows clearly how deceptive is our view of the sky. In this respect, this atlas attempts to harmonize the apparent and the real.

If we look once more at Fig. 1, we will see that the star δ Cas is brighter than ε Cas. Measurements, however, have disclosed that the reason that the latter is fainter is that it is further away from the Earth. On the other hand, γ Cas is much further away and yet is the brightest of all the stars in the W. This shows that a star's brightness is not always determined by its diameter but by the fact that it has a higher surface temperature.

Reality or Illusion

Of great interest is the question of the stars' visibility. In fact we do not actually see the stars' surfaces; at such great distances they are too small to be perceived as objects by the naked eye. What we do see is merely the so-called diffraction image in our eye, or in the optical instrument being used, of the light from the star; thus all that we know is ascertained by analyzing this light. Part of this radiation, however, is absorbed by the Earth's atmosphere, and furthermore the eye is more sensitive to the red end of the spectrum than to the blue. This partially explains the surprising fact that in the reports of astronauts who have made flights into space there are no enthusiastic references to any great increase in the number of visible stars; this fact is borne out by the photographs made of the sky by space probes. In any case it is to be expected that the visibility of stars in space will in no way differ from their visibility on Earth under ideal conditions, e.g. in the mountains or in the tropics. Theoretically, the stars should be brighter because light absorption is eliminated. But experience reveals that when viewed from a mountain observatory located at an elevation of 1800 metres (5600 feet) their visibility is practically the same as when viewed from an elevation of 3000 metres (9400 feet).

We seldom realize that the only window through which we can view stellar space at all is the shadow cast by the Earth. Because the Sun is much larger than the Earth, this shadow is comparatively short and thin, surrounded on all sides by bright sunlight. The Earth's rapid rotation is a great asset to astronomers for it enables them to view a large part of stellar space daily. At the Equator it can even be viewed in its entirety from a single place once a day.

The absurdity of it all is that during his investigations of the stars, man is not standing on an immovable foundation as he tends to suppose, but hangs attached to the Earth's sphere like steel filings stuck to a huge magnet suspended in an infinite void. In addition to this, the Earth is not motionless but is turning, so that new stars are continually appearing on the horizon. Despite these complications man has succeeded in learning much about the stars.

Brief Account of the Measurement of Stellar Distances

Determining stellar distances has always been one of the more difficult tasks of astronometry, because the angles measured are so small — mere hundredths and thousandths of a second of arc. Measurements are based on the apparent, annual, pendulum-like motion of the star whose distance is being measured against the background of other, fainter stars located further from the Sun, it being assumed or known that their own relative motion will not affect the accuracy of the measurement. The distance of the star is determined by the trigonometric method commonly used by cartographers and geodesists for measuring distant objects on the Earth's surface. This method consists in sighting the object from the two ends of a baseline and determining its parallax, which is expressed as the difference of the angles in fractions of minutes or seconds of arc. From the length of the baseline and the amount of parallax observed, the distance of the object can be calculated. In astronomy the baseline is formed by the two ends of the diameter of the Earth's orbit around the Sun, and the distance is stated in light years. This baseline was first used for measurement by Frederick Bessel, the famous German mathematician and astronomer, who, after a year of observations of the star 61 Cygni, announced its distance in 1838. In 1839 Henderson ascertained that the distance of α Centauri is $4\frac{1}{3}$ light years, which has proved to be the closest of all the stars (except the Sun); and by the end of the nineteenth century fifty-five parallaxes had been determined by the trigonometric method.

A further step forward in the determination of stellar distances was the introduction of the photographic method in 1904. The use of a high-powered telescope with a long focus increased the precision and number of parallax measurements, so that by the mid-twentieth century they already numbered 5822. These measurements have been made many times and subjected to detailed scrutiny to eliminate any possible mistakes. The Yale Observatory in the United States published the first catalogue of these stars. This classic list also serves as a reference for the description of the stars in this atlas.

Objects in the Sky

Star Clusters

Not all stars are solitary, isolated occupants of space; many exist in large associations bound to each other by the force of gravity. These associations are known as star clusters. Some contain only a few stars; but in others enormous numbers are collected together. In some groups it can be assumed that all the members came into being at the same time, this being borne out by the similarities in visual magnitude, distance and spectral class. Astronomers distinguish the following four types of star clusters:

1. *Open Star Clusters* — characteristic and very abundant in the Galactic plane, in the Magellanic Clouds and in the arms of numerous galaxies. Typical open clusters are the Pleiades, the Praesepe Cluster in Cancer, the Double Cluster χ and h Persei, the clusters in Auriga and in many other places. Clusters can also be differentiated by the age of their stars. In some the majority are relatively new stars with high temperatures whereas in others orange and red giants predominate.

2. *Globular Star Clusters* — distinguished chiefly by the vast number of stars associated in a stellar conglomeration of spherical shape. These contain some 10,000 to 10,000,000 stars apparently concentrated toward the centre. Only two globular clusters are visible with the naked eye — M 13 in Hercules in the northern sky and ω Centauri in the southern hemisphere. At present about 120 globular star clusters are known. They contain a large number of variable stars.

3. *Moving Star Clusters* — these include relatively near stars scattered over the heavens. They comprise

some of the stars of the Great Bear and others that have approximately the same motion and velocity.

4. *Stellar Associations* — these are loose concentrations of hot stars of relatively short duration, estimated at about one million years. Most of the stars in Orion together with those of the Trapezium in the Great Nebula form such an association.

Nebulae and Galaxies

Nebulae are enormous clouds of gas and dust. Visible nebulae derive their luminosity from nearby hot stars, e.g. the North American Nebula in Cygnus. In some instances, such as in the Rosette Nebula in Monoceros, the gaseous parts of the nebula are excited to fluorescence by the presence of high-energy stars. A special group contains the so-called dark nebulae, known from photographs made in red light. These are clouds of gas and dust which are not excited to luminosity, and we see them as dark areas which obscure other stars from view. A classic example is the dark Horse-head Nebula in Orion.

Galaxies are numerically abundant objects lying outside the boundaries of the Milky Way. They are independent islands in various stages of evolution. These galaxies are classified by astronomers as elliptical, spiral and barred spiral types, and numerous further sub-classes of these groups. The galaxy closest to the Earth is the Great Nebula in Andromeda. The observation of galaxies requires a large astronomic telescope to resolve their structure. The amateur is generally disappointed by their appearance, which is much better revealed by photography with powerful instruments. For that reason this book has limited itself to the most prominent ones which the amateur may encounter in his perusal of popular scientific journals and publications.

Planetary Nebulae

These have nothing in common with the planets of the solar system except the name, which was given to them in the eighteenth century because they appear as small, faintly glowing discs resembling the distant planets, in particular Uranus.

Planetary nebulae are early types with a very high-temperature star (50,000 °K to 100,000 °K) at the centre, the strong emission of gases causing a loss of matter which envelops the star, sometimes in the shape of a regular sphere, at other times a simple or complex

Fig. 2 Schema of the Galaxy

All the stars we see in the sky belong to a large stellar island called *the Galaxy*. This island comprises more than 150,000 million stars and resembles a lens-shaped disc measuring 100,000 light years in diameter. Fig. 2 shows a schematic picture of our Galaxy. At the top the Galaxy is shown in profile; the spherical shape of the Galactic nucleus is clearly visible, and so is the region of dark interstellar matter obscuring the stars in the Galactic plane. The large dots denote the globular star clusters in the spherical cloud round the nucleus.

Viewed in plan (bottom illustration) we see that the stars round the galactic nucleus are arranged in the form of spiral arms. The Sun lies in close proximity to such an arm at a distance of 27,000 light years from the nucleus. The position of the Sun is indicated by a circle. The size of the circle corresponds to a diameter of 6000 light years — it is in this region that almost all the stars delineating the constellations and visible with the unaided eye are located. The other arms of the Galaxy are seen as the hazy silvery band of the Milky Way, which only a telescope will resolve into individual stars.

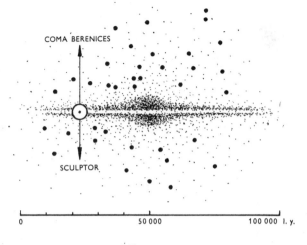

COMA BERENICES

SCULPTOR

0   50 000   100 000 l. y.

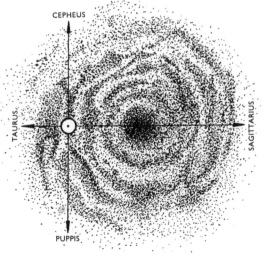

CEPHEUS

TAURUS.

SAGITTARIUS

PUPPIS

Fig. 2 Schema of the Galaxy.   29

ring. This matter is extremely tenuous, its density being a thousandth to a tenth that of the solar body. Everything points to the fact that the life of planetary nebulae is of relatively short duration, only several tens of thousands of years. In some examples the gaseous envelope has almost disappeared. At the present time, more than 1000 planetary nebulae are known, but the majority are very faint and their angular measure is so small that they cannot be distinguished from ordinary stars. The brightest planetary nebulae are the Dumb-bell in Vulpecula, and Saturn (so called because of its resemblance to that planet) and Hellix in Aquarius. Less bright is the Owl Nebula in Ursa Major.

Local Group of Galaxies

This term is applied to the objects located beyond the boundary of the Milky Way and closest to the Earth. These include the Magellanic Clouds, the Great Nebula in Andromeda, M 32 and NGC 205 Andromedae, and the Sculptor and Fornax systems.

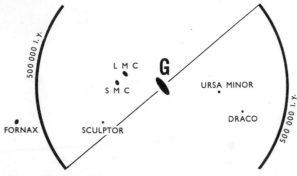

Fig. 3 The Neighbourhood of Our Galaxy.

Double Stars

Mention has been made of star clusters which are associations of vast numbers of stars, but there are also isolated double stars or multiple-star systems. Their number is by no means small, and astronomers therefore distinguish the following main types:

1. Optical Doubles appear to be double stars, i.e. the two stars appear to be close to each other, but in reality they are not. They only appear so because they lie near the same line of sight from the observer; in other words, through an accident of perspective, they are seen as doubles.

2. Close Doubles and Visual Doubles — the former, the close double, denotes that a telescope with greater magnification is required for resolution of the two stars than in the case of the latter, the visual double, which can be resolved with a smaller telescope. Their visibility depends on the size of the instrument employed and on the separation of the two components, which changes from one year to the next because of their revolution. The point on the elliptic orbit at which

Fig. 3   The Neighbourhood of Our Galaxy

Galaxies are fundamental stellar systems in space. Five are known to us up to a distance of 500,000 light years. These include the Magellanic Clouds (SMC and LMC), Ursa Minor, Sculptor and Draco. The letter G marks our Galaxy, which is the largest of the whole group. From the viewpoint of astronomy, this of course encompasses only our immediate surroundings. Today modern telescopes penetrating to distances measuring many thousands of millions of light years are observing systems of galaxies which in some parts of the sky exceed the number of stars visible with a normal telescope.

the two stars are closest to each other is called the *periastron*, and the point at which they are farthest apart is called the *apoastron*.

3. *Spectroscopic Doubles* are detected only from the displacement of the lines of the spectrum of the primary star. Visual separation of the two components is impossible. One example of such a complex system is the star Castor in Gemini.

The number of double and single stars in the sky is about equal. Each year new doubles, mostly spectroscopic, are added to the list. Of the 254 stars less than 10 parsecs distant from the Sun, 127 are members of 61 double and multiple systems. In the accompanying constellation maps reference is made only to those that are the most easily resolved. The only complex double systems visible with the unaided eye in the northern hemisphere are Alcor and Mizar in Ursa Major.

Variable Stars and Novae

Variable stars are stars whose brightness varies periodically, or which appear and after a short time again disappear. Because there was no explanation for such natural phenomena in the past, such stars were termed 'Wonderful' (Mira Ceti), or 'Demon' (Algol in Perseus). The appearance of a 'new star' was a rare occurrence and often escaped the notice of both simple folk and astronomers. If conditions were favourable and the new star very bright, it was usually considered to be primarily of astrological significance.

The progress made by astronomy in the nineteenth and twentieth centuries enabled hypotheses on the causes of these variations in light to be made. These causes can be divided roughly into two groups. The large number of variables known as eclipsing variables are double stars where one component eclipses the other for a time during each revolution. This period of eclipse is termed the minimum, the period when the star regains its original brightness being termed the maximum. Variations of this kind are many, and occur where the stars are oval in shape or where there is a difference in the inclination of their orbital plane.

Another reason for the light variation of variable stars is to be sought in the variations in the extent of the hot stellar atmosphere or of the stars' pulsation. These stars suddenly blaze brightly, but fade just as quickly. The reason for this may be an explosive outburst of the star's gaseous envelope.

Supernovae are extreme and rare cases of sudden outbursts with a range of more than 20 magnitudes in brightness. Classic examples are Kepler's supernova of 1604 at the foot of Ophiuchus and the supernova that appeared in 1054, the remains of which are the Crab Nebula in Taurus, of which mention has already been made.

Novae is the Latin name for stars increasing in brightness by 1 to 16 magnitudes. In some cases it was discovered that the star was one that had escaped notice before its sudden outburst. One such star was Nova Aquilae of 1918, and another was Nova Persei of 1901.

Recurrent Novae are novae with amplitude between the 7th and 9th magnitude that have experienced two or more outbursts.

The above is a general description of the characteristics of variable stars. More than 15,000 have been catalogued to date; and so it is quite inaccurate, as one can see, to refer to the light of the stars as being 'steady'. Further reference to variable stars will be found in the text accompanying the constellation maps, insofar as they are visible to the naked eye.

There is only one more fact that should be noted in this connection and that is how variable stars are designated in astronomic literature. The German astronomer Argelander used the capital letters of the Roman alphabet, beginning with R, placed before the name of the constellation to which the variable belongs, e.g. R Cygni. When this series is exhausted in any given constellation, double letters are used, e.g. RR Cygni, RR Lyrae, etc.

Systematic observation of variable stars by amateur methods is of little significance in the present day, but it is an interesting pursuit. The maps in this atlas show only those variables that attain at least 5th magnitude at the maximum.

Shooting Stars and Meteors

Shooting stars, as they are commonly called, are a well-known phenomenon of the skies. They consist generally of small fragments of loose matter, either stone or metal, known in scientific terminology as *meteors*. Brilliant shooting stars moving at a relatively slow speed are called *bolides*, or popularly, *fireballs*. The word 'meteor' (from the Greek for 'things on high') has the same root as 'meteorology', the science that deals with weather and weather forecasting; and it used to be thought that meteors were among the phenomena that influence the weather.

In former times, astronomers did not pay much attention to flights of meteors. People viewed them as a threat from the heavens and only exceptionally great numbers of shooting stars provoked interest, for they were then usually linked with some important event on Earth. From time to time, however, philosophers gave explanations that came very close to those of today. For instance Anaxagoras, when he learned of the fall of a meteor in Thrace, proclaimed that it had fallen from the Sun. Plutarch believed that these objects came from the skies and fell not only on land but into the sea as well.

It was not till the eighteenth century, however, that a physicist, the Austrian Chladni, had the courage to proclaim that the origin of meteors must be sought in interplanetary space. In 1798 two German students at the University of Göttingen simultaneously observed shooting stars from two distant points in order to determine their parallax, thus obtaining the necessary data for determining the height at which the meteors appeared. They correctly assumed that the path of one and the same meteor would be viewed differently from each of the two points. N. A. Newton, on the basis of twenty-one observed and charted paths, calculated that meteors travel at a height of approximately 61 miles, thus ascertaining at the same time the height of the Earth's atmosphere and the speed at which meteors penetrate its denser layers. These data have since been determined with greater accuracy.

On some nights meteors are seen in great numbers, appearing to emanate from a single point which is called the *radiant*. They give the impression of shooting out fanwise from this point over the sky. This is an illusion caused by perspective distorting reality, just as railway tracks, or trees lining a long straight road, appear to converge in the distance. Modern science knows that meteor showers are closely related to the paths of comets and that when the Earth's orbit intersects or approaches these paths, the showers are particularly strong. The meteor streams are named after the constellations from which they appear to come, e.g. the Perseids, Leonids, Lyrids, or after the cometary fragments with which they are associated, e.g. the

MAJOR METEOR STREAMS

Name	Date of Appearance	Associated with Comet	Description
Lyrids	April 12 to 24 Max. April 22	Halley's Comet	At one time a rich stream but now less strong.
η Aquarids	April 29 to May 21 Max. May 5		A rich stream, better visible in the southern hemisphere.
δ Aquarids	June 25 to Aug 19 Max. July 30		Second encounter with foregoing stream.
Perseids	July 20 to Aug 19 Max. Aug 11	Tuttle's Comet of 1862 III	Once a strong stream, now becoming weaker.
Orionids	Oct 11 to 30 Max. Oct 19	Halley's Comet	A fairly active stream.
Taurids	Oct 24 to Dec 10 Max. Nov 13	Temple's Comet of 1866 I	Once a stream with very high rate of shooting stars, now much less active.
Geminids	Dec 5 to 19 Max. Dec 12		

Giacobinids and Bielids, and the richness of the display depends on the number of meteors entering the Earth's atmosphere. In many instances the cometary orbit on which the meteors travel is known and hence also their origin. Astronomers distinguish meteor systems into *permanent* ones whose activity is constant, e.g. the Perseids, and *periodic* streams whose activity varies over given periods. If the orbit of a given stream is only at a slight angle to the ecliptic, the Earth encounters it twice a year; such showers are called *ecliptical streams*. Some meteors and radiants are *sporadic*, i. e. they appear outside known radiants. Besides these there are also the *telescopic meteors* whose numbers are determined by the number that pass through the field of view of a telescope.

Meteor streams can now be observed in broad daylight by radar. Their trail is detected by radar equipment which records the exact time of their passage and other data. The participation of amateurs in the observation of meteor streams is possible and often useful. Much depends on the organization and perseverance of the group and on its equipment, especially photographic and chronometric apparatus, but most important of all is the way of treating these observations.

From Theory to Practice

Amateur astronomers are to be found the world over in every class of society. Some are satisfied with occasional observations of the heavens. Others wish to probe more deeply, and the results of their work can at times be compared with those of a professional. This however is not the rule, for such results arise from extensive knowledge, long experience and the opportunity of working with large and intricate instruments. The amateur who has limited funds can extend his observations by purchasing at least a small telescope. In addition, however, it is necessary to train the eye to observe and notice minute details, as well as to have a knowledge and understanding of celestial objects, and not to expect to see all the spectacular phenomena one is accustomed to seeing in photographs. The eye has the unique ability of adapting itself to great light contrasts and seeing minute details at the same time. However, the picture it sees vanishes the instant the eye is removed from the eyepiece and whatever we attempt to draw on paper is uncertain and deceptive. Photography, on the other hand, has the advantage of permanently registering the image of the observed object.

Except in the case of the Moon, a small telescope reveals little of permanent interest to the observer, but a telescope with greater magnification will give much pleasure to the amateur who can afford it and who has a suitable place to mount it. Such an instrument cannot be held in the hand; it requires a special steady support with a parallactic mounting equipped with a clockwork drive. This alone will guarantee steady observation from the Earth which is in constant rotation. It is also possible for the amateur to make a telescope himself, but this requires some mechanical training plus the facilities of an optical workshop. Some communities have observatories that are open to the public, where from time to time the amateur can observe interesting objects in the sky with a really large telescope. Such observatories or astronomical societies arrange courses in observation and these are strongly recommended to the amateur, who will gain much valuable experience from them.

Sky Maps and Atlases

To find one's way around the stellar sphere and to learn the various constellations would seem to be an almost impossible feat, but in reality it is perhaps no more difficult than learning to read music. All that is required is patience and good sky maps, which can be read as easily and can yield as much information as maps of the Earth's surface. With a good atlas and a little imagination, one can set out on distant journeys, learning about the mountains, rivers, cities, and people in far-off lands without the least hope of ever coming to know them in person. The same applies to maps of heavens. Ever since remote times, scholars have wanted to record the knowledge they have gained from observation of the celestial sphere. Thus the first star atlases came into existence, their rich ornamentation being inspired primarily by the symbolism of the stars' names.

The history of star atlases is for the most part fairly recent, dating from the early seventeenth century when the technique of printing was perfected. Their precursors were made from woodcuts. The first star atlases were not only sources of information but also works of art. A classic is the atlas entitled *Uranometria* published in 1603 by Johann Bayer, an advocate in Augsburg. The constellations were depicted by artistic symbolic figures which were adopted by almost all subsequent maps of the celestial sphere. Some of these pagan figures, however, were not in accord with the views of the day, and attempts were often made to replace the old figures by new ones. Even during Bayer's lifetime (and with his aid) we find Julius Schiller publishing a new atlas under the title *Coelum Stellarum Christianum*, in which the old names of the constellations were supplanted by new ones better suited to the Christian idea of the heavens, the twelve Signs of the Zodiac for instance being assigned the names of biblical figures, e.g. St. Paul instead of Perseus, the Three Magi instead of Hercules, etc. But despite the fine engravings the book was not a success. The *Atlas Coelestis* (1729) of John Flamsteed (1646—1719) was another finely illustrated production. The year 1801 marked the publication of *Uranographia*, which contains magnificent maps by the famous astronomer John Elert Bode and is a supreme work of its kind. Although other star atlases were published in the nineteenth century, none attained the artistic merit of Bode's for the simple reason that, with the evolution of astronomy and increasing knowledge, atlases with artistic decoration became an anachronism. Scientifically their chief drawback was the non-uniformity of the boundaries of the constellations, which were delineated more or less capriciously. This caused confusion and uncertainty in the identification of fainter stars, and it became obvious that the establishment of a unified system was sorely needed. John Herschel (1792—1871) suggested that the old symbols of the constellations be preserved but that the sky be

40

divided into spherical quadrangles regardless of the former boundaries, and that these areas be named Regio Leonis, Regio Virginis, etc. This progressive idea, however, was not accepted, and it was not till 1927 that the International Astronomical Union adopted the suggestion of the Belgian astronomer E. Delporte that the arbitrary boundaries be defined by hour angle and declination. The Delporte boundaries are used in this atlas.

Today's amateur astronomer has many aids to help him find his way in the sky, ranging from small atlases to detailed scientific books. Widely used are the *Tabulae Coelestes* by Schurig-Götz, Norton's *Star Atlas*, and Delporte's *Atlas Celeste* (Cambridge University Press, 1930), which contain much clear information and are of suitable size for direct observation of the sky. They are inadequate, however, for the advanced amateur, who will find the *Atlas Coeli* by Dr Antonín Bečvář better suited for this purpose. This atlas comprises sixteen large-size maps showing the whole northern and southern hemispheres with stars of apparent magnitude down to 7.5, star clusters, nebulae and galaxies down to the 13th magnitude. They also show variable stars of all types, double stars, novae, radiants and cosmic radiation sources. A supplement to this atlas is a catalogue containing more detailed data on all the objects shown on the maps. These two volumes (the maps and the catalogue) served as the source material for all the data contained in this book.

Planispheres are often obtainable for local use; these facilitate the determination of the constellations visible above the horizon at a given instant. Such a device is a valuable aid, but it can be used only in that geographical latitude for which it is intended.

The amateur can derive much help from the various

astronomical year-books which contain information on all phenomena in the sky for a given year. The amateur will find popular scientific magazines a better source than books for acquiring quickly knowledge of the latest developments in astronomy. Scientific books, of course, are an important part of the amateur's library, for they contain the basic theories that form the foundations of present-day astronomy. These books may be supplemented by dictionaries of astronomy that give brief definitions of the terms the amateur needs to know and use for his observations.

What Can We See with Binoculars?

The human eye can distinguish comparatively few objects in the sky apart from the stars, Moon and planets. The reason for this is the limited sensitivity of the eye and the small apparent magnitude of the majority of distant objects. We know from the literature that outer space is filled with a vast number of gaseous nebulae, galaxies and star clusters. The brighter ones are generally shown on maps, and identified with the numbers under which they are listed in scientific catalogues. Two such catalogues are in common use today. The first, dating from the late eighteenth century and containing 119 nebulae and star clusters, was compiled by the French astronomer Charles Messier, observer of comets, and therefore all the numbers in his catalogue are prefixed by the capital letter M. Thus the Great Nebula in Andromeda is designated M 31. Some astronomers prefer to use the other designation assigned to this nebula, namely NGC 224, these letters being an abbreviation of the title of the vast *New General Catalogue*, which is supplemented by the IC or *Index Catalogue*. Messier's catalogue limits itself to the brighter objects in the sky, and that is why its numbers frequently appear on the maps of this book.

Open Star Clusters are associations of brighter stars, relatively distant from each other, but bound by gravitational force. Typical examples in the northern sky are the Pleiades and Hyades in Taurus. Clearly visible to the naked eye is the Praesepe Cluster in Cancer. The brightest cluster in the southern hemisphere is the Jewel Box. Less bright is the Double Cluster χ and h Persei between Cassiopeia and Perseus. Many open star clusters are to be found in the Milky Way, chiefly in Sagittarius, Ophiuchus and in the small constellation Scutum. Opera glasses will reveal small star clusters in numerous other parts of the sky as well. These are marked on the maps of this atlas.

Globular Clusters are distinguished from open clusters by the greater density of their seemingly minute members. The concentration at the centre is so great that only a few can be resolved with a larger telescope. The unaided eye can barely distinguish three of the whole number. One such well-known cluster is M 13 in Hercules. Its total brightness is of the 6th magnitude, which is on the treshold of naked eye visibility. More easily distinguished are the globular clusters ω Centauri and 47 Tucanae occupying an area of the celestial sphere equal to that of the full Moon. Viewed through a large telescope the three clusters are truly magnificent. They are a system of suns bound by great gravitational force. We know of course that the apparent closeness of these suns to one another is caused by their vast distance from the Earth, for the conglomeration as a whole measures from 15 to 120 parsecs and contains several hundred thousand members. At present only slightly more than 120 globular clusters are known and it is presumed that the whole Galactic system contains about 220. These star systems are also known to exist in other galaxies, for example in the Great Nebula in Andromeda. The most difficult objects for an amateur to observe are the planetary nebulae which basically are gaseous envelopes surrounding very hot stars. They are usually round discs resembling the planets of the solar system, hence their name. Besides occurring as gaseous spheres they may also form complex rings. Planetary nebulae are very faint objects and are difficult to distinguish with small telescopes. They are better observed from photographs made with large reflectors and are known in literature under such names as the Crab Nebula in Taurus, the Owl Nebula in Ursa Major, the Ring Nebula in Lyra, the Dumb-bell in Vulpecula, Saturn and Hellix in Aquaris. Hellix is the largest and brightest of them all.

Diffuse Gaseous Nebulae occur predominantly in the southern hemisphere. Even though they occupy a large area in the sky, they are not, with two exceptions, suitable objects for observation with prismatic binoculars. The constellation Sagittarius contains several small clouds of the Trifid Nebula and the Lagoon Nebula, but these will hardly attract the novice who knows them from photographs and cannot himself see all the details they depict. Near the centre of the southern sky at coordinate 05h 39m and declination −69°04' lies the bright Tarantula gaseous nebula in Dorado. Far better known, however, is the nebula in Orion located below the three bright stars in the Belt of Orion and plainly visible to the naked eye. It is marked in the relevant map as M 42. The first written record about this nebula was made by G. B. Cysat in 1618, though it was known to many with good eyesight even before the discovery of the telescope. For three centuries numerous attempts were made to depict it on paper but none met with success. The drawings were the result of subjective observations and differed widely from each other, thus precluding any possibility of scientific study of its structure. It was not till 1888 that the nebula was first photographed, its spectrograms determined, and thus the foundations laid for its physical study. Four very hot stars known as the Trapezium are in the midst of the nebula. The distance of the Orion Nebula has not been exactly determined as yet, but is estimated to be 1700 light years and this figure seems to be the minimum. The diameter is 5 parsecs, the apparent diameter being about four times the apparent diameter of the full Moon.

Galaxies. The amateur will have little luck with the vast number of known galaxies, for all except one are faint objects of less than 7th magnitude, which is the limit of visibility with small prismatic binoculars. The one exception which can be viewed with the unaided eye on a clear night is the Great Nebula in Andromeda. Its existence was known to the ancients, but the first written report was made by the Persian astronomer Al Sufi in the tenth century. In December 1612 it was described by the German astronomer Simon Marius. With a small telescope he observed its bright nucleus and the hazy conical arms on either side. He compared their glow to the light of a candle passing through a thin horn plate. Many years have elapsed since then and it would seem that repetition of such classic observations could not yield different results. This however is not the case. Several years ago Robert Jonckheer made an interesting experiment at the Observatoire de Marseille. He wanted to discover the effect of external conditions on average eyesight. He used a binocular prism telescope with fifty-fold magnification having the optical surface treated with an anti-reflection coating. The eyepieces were carefully centred so as to make full use of both pupils at maximum aperture. Immediately before the experiment Jonckheer spent ten minutes in complete darkness. He also took the necessary precautions not to be disturbed by stray light when he looked through the binocular. A calm, clear and moonless night was chosen for the experiment.

The results were surprising. It was discovered that the longitudinal axis of the nebula measures 5°10′, in other words that it occupies an area in the sky more than ten times the apparent diameter of the full Moon, and that the shorter axis measures 1°05′. The measurements were checked with the stars in the vicinity of the nebula. This was truly an unexpected discovery, for all prior estimates had been much smaller. Jonckheer also discovered that the nucleus is located closer to the arm's northern tip.

The great spiral galaxy in Andromeda (M 31 or NGC 224) is known to be 2,300,000 light years distant, and has two companions, the nebulae NGC 205 and M 32 or NGC 221.

This concludes the list of objects visible with prismatic binoculars. The number of course increases with the increasing size and light-gathering power of the telescope employed. With good optical aids the amateur can venture on clear nights into the world of comets. Their location and observation require patience and perseverance; the cloud amidst the stars that appears in the telescope's field of view must not be mistaken for a known nebula or globular star cluster.

Where, When and How to Find Celestial Objects

The Constellations

There are different ways of going about finding and distinguishing the various constellations in the sky. The novice is best advised to have someone versed in the subject point out at least the better known constellations such as Ursa Major, Cassiopeia, Orion, Scorpius, etc. In this way he will acquire several starting points from which he can set out to explore nearby areas with the aid of star maps showing the positions of the constellations (pages 75 to 85). We proceed along the line connecting two known stars and extend it in the direction of the constellation we are seeking, first on the map, and then in the sky, with the help of angular measurements (see page 70).

Let us suppose that all the constellations are attached to a huge, hollow sphere — the celestial sphere. Slowly revolving in the centre of that sphere is a small ball — the Earth — and at some point on that Earth stands an inquisitive person scanning the sky. The Earth under his feet is so large that it conceals one whole half of the celestial sphere. What will he see in the other half of that sphere above the horizon?

The Earth is round and each observer sees different stars when he looks up at the sky above his head (the zenith): A, who lives in the northern hemisphere, will see above his head the Great Bear (UMA). C, in the southern hemisphere, will see the Southern Cross (CRU) when he looks up, but he can never see the Great Bear from his point of observation. B, with Cassiopeia (CAS) at the zenith, is on the same geographical latitude as A but on the opposite meridian,

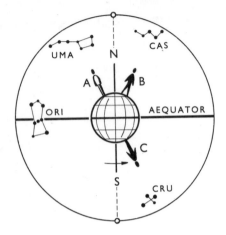

Fig. 4

so he will find himself under the Great Bear 12 hours later as a result of the Earth's rotation. Each of the three, A, B and C, can occasionally see the constellation Orion (ORI) which lies above the equator. (Fig. 4)

The geographical latitude of the place of observation more or less determines which stars we shall be able to observe. Geographical latitude on the ground corresponds to the declination in the sky. The terrestrial equator has its counterpart in the celestial equator, which is a great imaginary circle dividing the sky into the northern and southern hemispheres. At the equator the declination is zero, north of this line it is positive and south of this line it is negative. Thus the 50th parallel northern latitude runs directly below the 50th parallel northern declination. If A were standing at the North Pole, then directly above his head would be the north celestial pole which has a declination of $+90°$. Declination is given in degrees on all the maps of this atlas. (Fig. 5)

Fig. 5

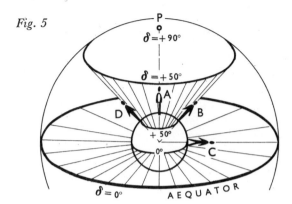

The declination helps to determine which part of the celestial sphere is visible to the observer. The

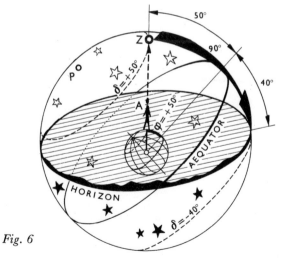

Fig. 6

following example will illustrate this more clearly. A is located at 50°N latitude (the longitude being irrelevant in this case). Directly above his head runs the 50th parallel northern declination (+50°). His zenith (Z) is therefore 50° from the celestial equator. The angle of the zenith to the horizon, as we know, is 90°. Therefore the position of the celestial equator above the horizon will be 90° — 50° = 40°. Thus A is able to see the whole northern hemisphere (from the equator to the pole P) plus the part of the southern hemisphere up to the 40th parallel southern declination (—40°). As the Earth rotates beneath the celestial vault, A is able to observe about three-quarters of the whole sphere in all. (Fig. 6)

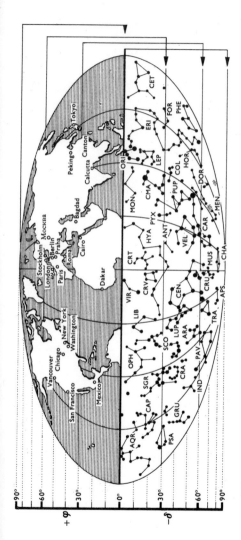

Fig. 7

How much of the southern celestial hemisphere below the equator can a northern observer see? This is determined by the distance from the latitude of his location to the South Pole, which has the southern most declination. From Cairo it is already possible to see part of the Southern Cross.

51

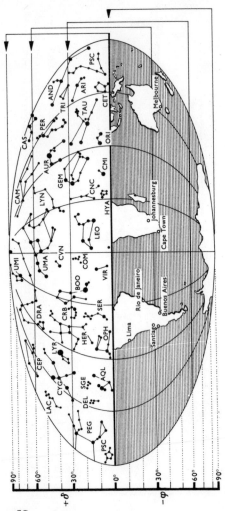

Fig. 8

The southern observer can view the whole of the southern hemisphere plus part of the northern hemisphere up to 90° north of the latitude of his location. From Capetown it is possible to see Leo and Gemini but only part of the Great Bear (Ursa Major).

Ideal conditions for observation are to be found at the equator, from where the whole heavens are visible from the north celestial pole to the south celestial pole. The Arctic and Antarctic regions offer the most restricted view. On the other hand, only at the North and South Poles is it possible to see at the same time all the constellations which can be viewed from those points. Elsewhere the observer moves with the Earth's rotation and views the constellations one after the other as they rise above the horizon. To find them he must first have a rough idea of celestial direction.

Let us consider the direction of the meridian. This is a very important circle in the sky; it passes above our heads (through the zenith Z) from the North (N) through the celestial pole (P) to the South Pole (S). It runs directly above our terrestrial meridian. The Sun is located on this meridian at midday. The direction of the meridian (north-south) is easily determined even at other times of the day with the aid of a compass or the hands of a watch. Point the small hand of the watch towards the Sun and divide the angle between the small hand and the number 12 in half; this bisecting line points to the meridian (m). (Fig. 9)

Fig. 9

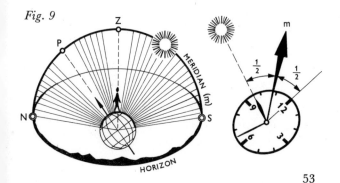

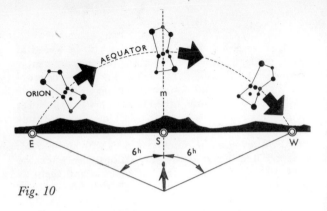

Fig. 10

It is on the meridian that the constellations culminate (reach their highest point in the heavens). Equatorial constellations, such as Orion, cross the meridian six hours after rising and set six hours later. The meridian is a sure guide in helping to locate constellations. (Fig. 10)

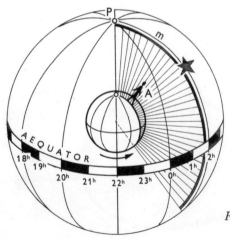

Fig. 11

Now let us learn how to recognize the position of the celestial sphere and the constellations in relation to the meridian passing through the point of observation. First imagine the celestial equator divided from a given point into 24 equal parts — hours — from west to east, thus dividing the sky like the dial of a clock with the meridian m serving as the hour hand. This 'clock' shows *sidereal time*. The dial looks like the edge of a huge open fan passing from one horizon through the meridian of our place of observation and stretching all the way to the other horizon. The sidereal time, of course, is different for each meridian. On the meridian of A's location it is 2 hours sidereal time. The star crossing the meridian at that instant has a *right ascension* of 2^h. Right ascension in the sky is the equivalent of the geographical longitude on the Earth. (Fig. 11)

The sky is the most accurate clock of all. Each star has its right ascension which gives the sidereal time at the instant the star crosses the meridian. If we know the sidereal time, then we know the position of the sky. For example at 6^h sidereal time Orion will always be on the meridian. (Fig. 12)

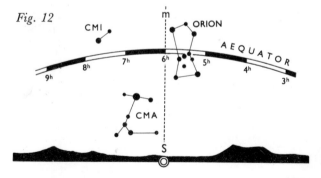

Fig. 12

55

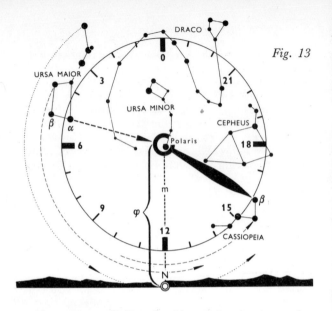

Fig. 13

How can we tell what the sidereal time is at our point of observation? Observatories have special clocks giving the sidereal time with great precision. For our purposes, however, the approximate sidereal time will suffice. This can be estimated by a glance at the sky. In the northern hemisphere locate the star β Cassiopeiae and connect it with Polaris, which we find with the aid of the Great Bear; this line is the hour hand of the sidereal clock whose dial is divided as shown in the illustration. With a little practice we shall soon be able to tell at least the hours on this clock.

One more item of information that will prove valuable is the fact that the altitude of Polaris, which lies close to the north celestial pole, is about equal to the geographical latitude of the point of observation. (Fig. 13)

Sidereal time can be accurately determined for any given day and hour with the aid of the diagram. This diagram is arranged as follows: the horizontal scale gives the date, the vertical scale the time (the standard time indicated on a 24 hour clock), and the diagonal scale the sidereal time.

Find the date on the horizontal scale (e.g. May 1) and draw a vertical line through this point. Then find the hour of observation (e.g. 20ʰ) on the vertical scale and draw a horizontal line through this point. The point of intersection of the two lines gives the sidereal

Fig. 14

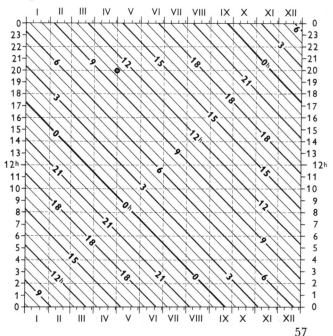

time on the diagonal scales (in this case approximately $10^h 30^m$). (Fig. 14)

Sidereal time tells us which constellations are crossing the meridian at a given instant. These are the constellations in which the right ascension of the stars is close to the sidereal time. The sidereal time will also enable us to estimate the approximate positions of other constellations. Right ascension is indicated in hours on all maps in this atlas.

Visibility of the constellations also depends on the time of the year, in other words on the location of the Sun amidst the stars.

On May 1 the Sun lies in the direction of the constellation Aries, which together with the neighbouring constellations is not visible at this time because they

Fig. 15

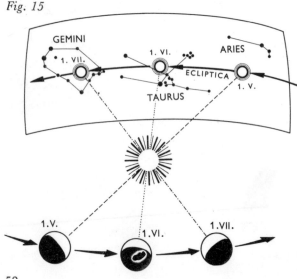

are above the horizon only in the daytime. One month later, i.e. on June 1, the point of observation has shifted and the Sun lies in the constellation Taurus. Thus the Sun appears to move from one constellation to another along a path called the *ecliptic*. The ecliptic passes through the twelve zodiacal constellations — the Ram (Aries), the Bull (Taurus), the Twins (Gemini), the Crab (Cancer), the Lion (Leo), the Virgin (Virgo), the Scales (Libra), the Scorpion (Scorpius), the Archer (Sagittarius), the Goat (Capricornus), the Water Carrier (Aquarius), and the Fishes (Pisces). (Fig. 15)

Because the Sun seemingly moves amongst the stars, the pattern of the sky changes during the year. Each

Fig. 16

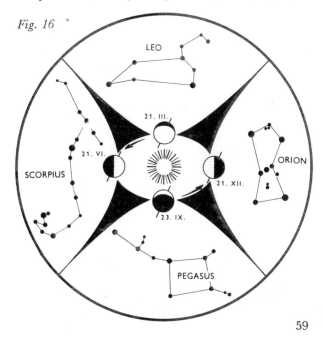

season has its typical constellations, which are visible almost the whole night long. These are the constellations that are located on the horizon opposite the Sun, e.g. the Lion in spring, the Scorpion in summer, Pegasus in autumn, and Orion in winter (this applies to the northern hemisphere; in the southern hemisphere the order is reversed). The four maps on pages 77 to 83 show the positions of the constellations during the four seasons of the year.(Fig. 16)

We have mentioned several ways of classifying the constellations. In relation to the celestial equator they are divided into three groups — the northern, southern and equatorial (the latter lie on the equator or in its immediate proximity). The eighty-eight constellations on the maps of this atlas have been classified accordingly with a coloured rectangle in the upper right-hand corner denoting the group to which each belongs (see explanations on page 88).

At the place of observation we divide them into *circumpolar* constellations — ones that never set — and *setting* constellations — ones that rise above the horizon for only a given time. Those in the remaining part of the celestial sphere are the *non-rising* constellations.

The constellations can also be divided into groups according to the season of the year, as we have already stated.

The Zodiac and the Planets

Of all the constellations those that lie along the ecliptic, that is the zodiacal family, have been the centre of interest since ancient times. This is not surprising for it is in this belt that the Sun, Moon and planets move, and it was according to the position of these bodies that ancient astrologers attempted to divine a person's future. About 2000 years ago they divided the ecliptic into twelve equal parts of 30° each, or twelve 'signs', to facilitate the determination of the location of the planets. The first sign, i.e. the first twelfth part of the ecliptic, began where the ecliptic intersects the celestial equator, the point where the Sun is located on March 21. This marks the beginning of spring in the northern hemisphere, and this point of intersection is called the *vernal equinox*, ('vernal' meaning 'of spring'). It is the 'first point of Aries' as it marks the beginning of that constellation*. Both the vernal equinox and the Ram have the same sign ♈, which is the symbol of the ram's horns. The symbols of all the zodiacal constellations are given in the following table:**

Aries (the Ram)	0° — 30°
Taurus (the Bull)	30° — 60°
Gemini (the Twins)	60° — 90°
Cancer (the Crab)	90° —120°
Leo (the Lion)	120° —150°
Virgo (the Virgin)	150° —180°
Libra (the Scales)	180° —210°
Scorpius (the Scorpion)	210° —240°
Sagittarius (the Archer)	240° —270°
Capricornus (the Goat)	270° —300°
Aquarius (the Water Carrier)	300° —330°
Pisces (the Fishes)	330° —360°

* and ** see page 62.

Fig. 17

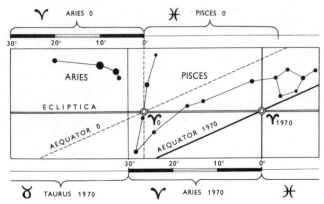

About 2000 years ago the signs lay in the constellations of the same name. The celestial equator, however, slowly shifts among the stars because of the Earth's precession, and so the vernal equinox and all the signs of the zodiac slowly move along the ecliptic, completing a full cycle once every 26,000 years. At the present time the vernal equinox is in Pisces and so is the sign of Aries. Naturally all the other signs are also one constellation behind, relative to the constellation of the same name. To this day, as in days of old, we say that on March 21 the Sun enters the sign of Aries, though in actual fact it is in the constellation Pisces. (Fig. 17)

---

* Beginning with the vernal equinox, the celestial equator is divided into 24 hours in right ascension. The vernal equinox plays the same role in the sky as Greenwich on the earth.

** The numbers in the table give the celestial longitude of the zodiacal constellations. The longitude is measured from the vernal equinox in the direction of the Sun's annual movement, from 0° to 360°.

The four maps of the ecliptical constellations (Fig. 18—21) show when the Sun enters the various signs (e.g. in Fig. 20 we find that on September 23 the Sun enters the sign of Libra).

The difference between the terms 'signs' and 'constellations' in the zodiac is best illustrated by the sign of Sagittarius, into which three constellations intrude, namely Scorpius, Ophiuchus (which now covers the greater part of the sign though it is not considered a zodiacal constellation) and Sagittarius.

The following maps will be particularly helpful in identifying the planets. We often notice that some of the zodiacal constellations contain a bright object which is not charted on the colour maps. In all probability it is one of the four bright planets, Venus, Mars, Jupiter or Saturn. We can see even Mercury with the unaided eye, but only on rare occasions and at twilight in the proximity of the Sun, when the constellations are beginning to appear in the darkening sky. We shall exclude also other objects such as airplanes, artificial satellites (these are identified by their motion) and novae, and shall limit ourselves to these four planets, whose astronomical symbols are as follows:

| ♀ | Venus | ♃ | Jupiter |
| ♂ | Mars | ♄ | Saturn |

Unlike the stars which appear to twinkle in the sky, the light from the planets is relatively steady. Another means of identifying them is by their colour and brightness.

Venus is a brilliant white and the brightest 'star' in the sky. Its brightness ranges between −3.5 and −4.3. It moves in the close vicinity of the Sun and appears at

63

dawn as the Morning Star and after sunset as the Evening Star. Its phases can be observed through a small telescope.

Mars is orange-red in colour. Its stellar magnitude ranges from $+1.5$ to -2.8, depending on its distance from the Earth.

Jupiter shines with a white light. It is always fainter than Venus but brighter than Sirius in Canis Major, the brightest actual star in the sky. The stellar magnitude is -1.6 to 2.3. Prismatic binoculars will disclose the brightest four moons of this planet.

Saturn is faintly yellowish and has a stellar magnitude $+0.9$ to -0.1. The famous rings of Saturn require a larger telescope to be visible.

The planets follow the path of the ecliptic and describe intricate paths against the stars, as the planets are revolving around the Sun and are viewed from the Earth, which is also moving around the Sun.

Easy identification of the planets and observation of their movements will be aided by the following four maps of the ecliptical constellations (pages 65 to 68) supplemented by tables of the planets' positions for the years 1970 to 1980. The tables give the positions of Venus, Mars, Jupiter and Saturn for the first day of every month. In some instances, chiefly for Saturn, some of the data are omitted for better clarity. Thus number 1 marks the position of the planet on the first of January, number 2 the position of the planet on the first of February, number 3 the position of the planet on the first of March, etc. Each planet is marked with a different type of numeral.

The point on the ecliptic located directly above a specific number marks the position of the given planet on the first day of the given month.

The planets generally follow the path of the ecliptic,

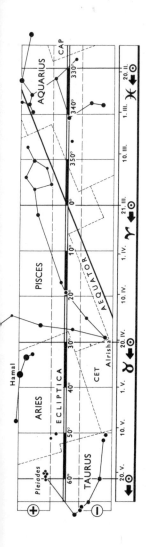

Fig. 18

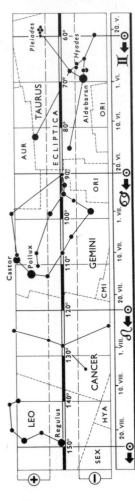

Fig. 19

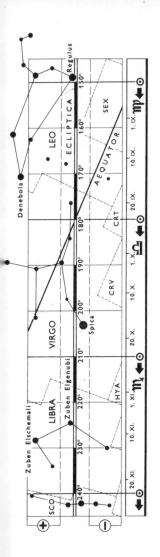

Fig. 20

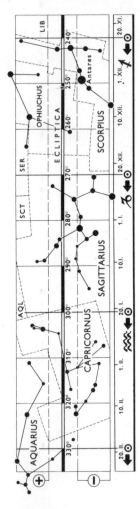

Fig. 21

moving in a belt measuring some 6° across. This 'celestial highway' is marked on the maps with a broken line. The only exceptions are Venus and Mars which sometimes move farther out or closer than 3° from the ecliptic in the bands marked + and −. In the tables this is marked with a + or − sign alongside the respective numeral-date.

Example: In the first table, line 1970, No. 5 denotes the position of Venus on 1 May 1970. On the top map we find that on that date Venus is in the constellation Taurus, at the left below the Pleiades.

On line 1972 the No. 4 has a + sign in front of it which means that on 1 April 1972 Venus will be on the line between Taurus and Aries, at the right above the Pleiades.

The tables will be a great help in following the direct counter-clockwise motion of the planets as well as their retrograde (clockwise) motion. Remember that the planets always move from the lower to the higher numbers. Mastery of the tables will even help in calculating the conjunction of planets.

Marked at the bottom of each map is the position of the Sun for every first, tenth and twentieth day of the month. The position of the Sun relative to that of a given planet on a given date will enable us to determine what the conditions for observation will be like, i.e. whether the planet will be visible in the evening or morning, etc.

One more example of interest: In 1974, sometime in December, it will be possible to observe a bright, approximately 1st magnitude star at the right below the bright stars Castor and Pollux in Gemini. Find this point on the map, run your finger down to the line marking the year 1974 and locate the closest number XII (December), revealing the presence of Saturn.

69

Size of Celestial Objects

Some constellations are small, e.g. Sagitta and Delphinus, whereas others such as Hydra and Eridanus are 'super-constellations' stretching over one quarter of the celestial sphere. This atlas devotes one page to each, regardless of its size. How, then, can we tell a constellation's true dimensions so as to be able to recognize it in the sky?

A reliable aid is provided by the coordinates. All the maps are marked with a network of coordinates, showing parallels of declination. These imaginary lines in the sky are spaced 10° apart and will stand us in good stead as a scale for estimating the true dimensions of the constellations. First, however, it is necessary to

Fig. 22.

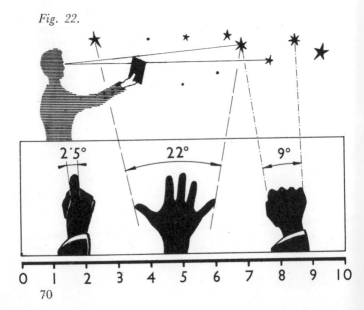

learn how to measure celestial objects or constellations in terms of *angles*, or *degrees of arc*.

We need neither sextant nor theodolite but only our hand plus a keen eye. If we hold a scale divided into sections of 0.89 centimetres in front of our eye at arm's length (a distance of 50 cm), each such section will correspond to one degree of arc in the sky. Such a scale is shown in Fig. 22, and on the back cover. With it we can determine what angles our thumb, fist, etc., cover in the sky when held out at arm's length.

Now try measuring the angular diameter of the Moon or the Sun. You may be surprised to discover that these objects can be covered by the little finger, for their diameter measures only 0.5°. Practise measuring with the hand or with the book on well-known constellations such as Ursa Major, Orion and the like; then when you locate a constellation for the first time you will be greatly aided by a correct estimate of its angular dimensions. If we learn the angular distances of certain stars, they, too, can serve as a scale; e.g. the separation between the rear stars of the Plough is 5°.

Sky Maps

The following six maps show the whole celestial sphere, both northern and southern skies, and together with the maps on the fly-leafs of this book show the positions of all eighty-eight constellations.

Constellations in the Region of the North Celestial Pole

The most prominent member of this group is the Great Bear (Ursa Major), part of which is the figure delineated by seven bright stars known as the Plough. It is a constellation that is familiar to all observers in the northern hemisphere and is the best starting point for the novice. The line connecting the star α (Dubhe) and β (Merak) points to the Pole Star (Polaris) in the Little Bear (Ursa Minor). The Pole Star lies less than 1° from the north celestial pole at the centre of the map. Stretching between the two bears is the Dragon (Draco).

If we extend the line from the Great Bear to the Pole Star the same distance beyond the pole, we encounter the five brightest stars in the Milky Way marking the W- or M-shaped figure of Cassiopeia, another of the familiar constellations in the northern sky. Between Cassiopeia and Draco lies Cepheus. This faint constellation has a shape resembling a child's drawing of a house. The Giraffe (Camelopardalis) and the Lynx (Lynx) are referred to by amateur astronomers as the 'invisible' constellations for they comprise very faint stars and can be seen only under ideal conditions.

Autumn Constellations

On this and the following three maps the constellations are divided according to the season of the year in which they are visible for the greater part of the night. This division into seasons applies to the northern hemisphere.

The northern observer finds his way among the stars by beginning with the square of Pegasus marked by the stars, α, β and γ in Pegasus and α in Andromeda. From the latter we proceed to β and γ Andromedae and thence to Algol in Perseus. The group of foregoing stars forms a figure resembling a large plough. South of Andromeda lie two small constellations: the Triangle (Triangulum) and the Ram (Aries).

The south-east apex of the square of Pegasus invades the broad V of the Fishes (Pisces), an inconspicuous constellation, as is the neighbouring Water Carrier (Aquarius), which is best recognized by its characteristic grouping of stars on the equator. Slightly more prominent is the Goat (Capricornus), lying on the ecliptic west of the triangular 'head' of Pegasus. The letter V in Pisces points like an arrow to the centre of the large constellation known as the Whale (Cetus).

In the southern hemisphere we shall first try to locate the brightest stars, namely Fomalhaut in the Southern Fish (Piscis Australis) and Achernar in Eridanus. The two together with Canopus in Carina (see map on the back fly-leaf) form a bright trio of stars lying approximately in a single straight line which will serve as a pointer in our journey among the stars. South of Fomalhaut lies the Crane (Grus), and close to Achernar lies the Phoenix (Phoenix). The faint constellations the Furnace (Fornax), the Sculptor (Sculptor), and the Microscope (Microscopium) can be located only under very good atmospheric conditions.

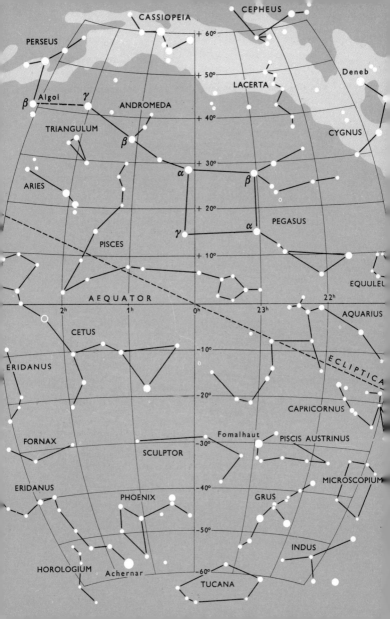

Winter Constellations

The winter sky is rich in bright stars, making it easy for the beginner to find his way.

One of the most striking figures in the heavens is Orion, whose brightest stars form a distinctive quadrangle with a trio of regularly spaced stars in the centre. The whole group resembles a butterfly with outspread wings. According to the original description of Orion as a hunter, this trio of stars is known as Orion's Belt. The northernmost star in the Belt lies close to the equator. Extended northward the Belt points toward the orange star Aldebaran in the Bull (Taurus). Following this line still further we encounter the bright group known as the Pleiades. Between the Pleiades and Cassiopeia (see map on front fly-leaf) lies the bridge formed by the arc of stars in Perseus. Nearby shines one of the brightest stars in the sky, namely Capella in the Charioteer (Auriga).

The line joining Rigel and Betelgeuse in Orion points to the Twins (Gemini), which is best fixed in one's mind by the two stars Castor and Pollux. Close to these lies the inconspicuous zodiac al constellation the Crab (Cancer).

According to mythology, Orion the hunter is followed by his two dogs, one large and one small. The Greater Dog (Canis Major) can be found by extending the line joining the stars of the Belt. The brightest star in the Greater Dog is Sirius, also the brightest star in the whole heavens. Between Sirius and Gemini lies the Lesser Dog (Canis Minor), with its bright star Procyon.

To facilitate his journey in the sky the beginner will find it wise to fix in his mind's eye the polygon formed by joining the following bright stars: Capella, Aldebaran, Rigel, Sirius, Procyon, Pollux and Castor.

Following the line south from Sirius along the band of the Milky Way we come to the Sail (Vela) and the Keel (Carina).

α Carinae (Canopus) is the second brightest star in the sky and is often used as a marker for navigation in space flights. From the star Rigel in Orion we can follow the meandering River (Eridanus) to the bright star Achernar.

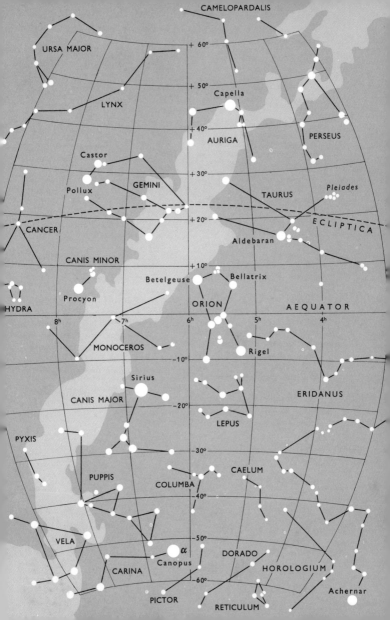

There are great differences between the southern and northern skies at this time of the year. Whereas the region near the equator and north of it is populated with very few bright stars, the sky near the southern pole provides a feast for the eyes.

In the north we shall start with the familiar seven bright stars marking the Plough in the Great Bear (Ursa Major). The line joining α and β of the Great Bear points to the Lion (Leo). The Lion is easily recognized by the group of stars resembling a large crescent or inverted question mark, and according to the original conception this denotes the lion's mane. Regulus, the brightest star in Leo, lies on the ecliptic. If we extend the handle of the Plough (tail of Ursa Major) along an arc to the equator, we shall encounter the orange star Arcturus in the Herdsman (Boötes). Farther along this arc below the equator we come to Spica in the Virgin (Virgo). The three stars Regulus, Arcturus and Spica form a large triangle which will serve as a useful guide in finding our way in the spring sky. Stretching below this triangle is the lengthy constellation the Water Snake (Hydra) whose 'head' lies below Cancer (see preceding map). Between Hydra and Virgo lies the small constellation known as the Crow (Corvus) and beside it the fainter Cup (Crater).

Lying in the Milky Way, which borders this whole region on the south, are the Sail (Vela) and the Keel (Carina). At the point where the two constellations touch there are four stars which form a cross, sometimes called the False Cross. The true Southern Cross (Crux) lies near the two bright stars α and β Centauri. This pair of stars not only points to the Southern Cross but also serves to identify the large constellation the Centaur (Centaurus).

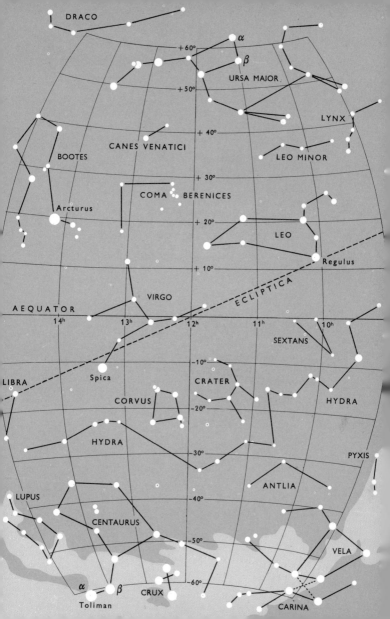

Summer Constellations

The shimmering band of the Milky Way will serve as a sure guide in finding the constellations of this part of the sky.

The northern observer will first of all look for the Summer Triangle formed by the bright stars Vega, Deneb and Altair. Blue-white Vega in the Lyre (Lyra) is one of the brightest stars in the heavens. Deneb lies in the tail of the Swan (Cygnus), which flies with widespread wings south along the Milky Way. Altair in the Eagle (Aquila) is accompanied on either side by fainter stars, rather like Orion's Belt. North of Altair lie two of the smallest constellations — the Dolphin (Delphinus) and the Arrow (Sagitta).

Close by Vega lie the head of the Dragon and the large constellation Hercules (Hercules), best remembered by thinking of it as a reversed K. Between Hercules and Boötes (see Spring Constellations) lies the Northern Crown (Corona Borealis) with the bright star Gemma. Below the Northern Crown is the Head of the Serpent (Serpens Caput), the serpent being held by the Serpent Holder (Ophiuchus). The Tail of the Serpent (Serpens Cauda) stretches all the way to the Eagle and extends into the two arms of the Milky Way.

Of the ecliptical (zodiacal) constellations, the most striking is the Scorpion (Scorpius) with its red star Antares. West of the Scorpion we find the Scales (Libra) and east of the Scorpion in the brightest part of the Milky Way, lies the Archer (Sagittarius). He is followed on the ecliptic by the Goat (Capricornus). Located south of the Archer is a regular crescent of faint stars marking the Southern Crown (Corona Australis). South of the Scorpion lies the clearly visible constellation the Altar (Ara), which resembles a simple drawing of an armchair. In the arm of the Milky Way between the Scorpion and Centaur we find the group of bright stars marking the Wolf (Lupus).

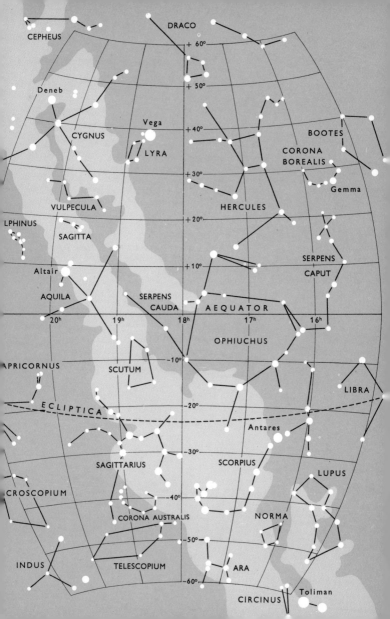

Constellations in the Region
of the South Celestial Pole

Finding our way in this part of the sky is somewhat more difficult than in the vicinity of the north pole, for the constellations here are generally faint.

The best place to start is with the Southern Cross (Crux) lying near the dark area in the Milky Way called the Coalsack. The brightest two stars in the Centaur point toward this cross, thus helping to distinguish it from the False Cross on the boundaries of the Sail and the Keel (see Spring Constellations). Smaller constellations near the Southern Cross are the Fly (Musca) with α Centauri and the Southern Triangle (Triangulum Australe) nearby.

There is no south star analogous to Polaris. Lying on the south celestial pole is the constellation the Octant (Octans), but it is very faint. The position of the pole can be determined with the help of the Southern Cross, whose longer arm points to it, or with the help of the Magellanic Clouds, which form a right-angled triangle with the pole. Both Magellanic Clouds (the Small Magellanic Cloud — SMC — and the Large Magellanic Cloud — LMC) are easily visible even when the Moon is shining.

A useful guide in the southern skies is the line joining the three bright stars Canopus in Carina, Achernar in Eridanus and Fomalhaut in Piscis Australis. On this line we can find the Painter's Easel (Pictor), the Goldfish (Dorado), the Net (Reticulum), the Pendulum Clock (Horologium) and the Phoenix (Phoenix). Of the other constellations in the vicinity of the pole we can locate the Peacock (Pavo) with comparative ease by its single bright star α Pavonis.

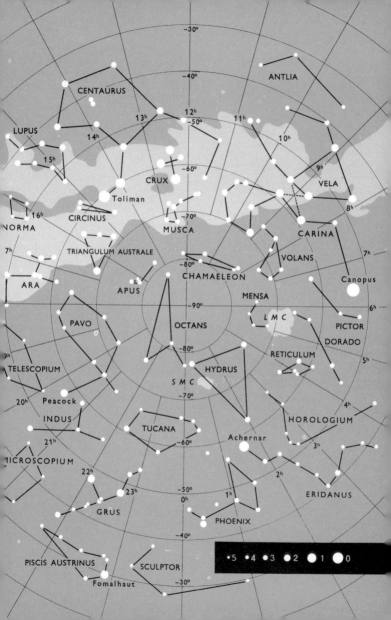

Constellation Maps

All data referred to in this book are taken from *Atlas Coeli* by Antonín Bečvář.
Through the ages, many stars have been given many different names, spelled or transliterated in many different ways. Some alternate spellings that might be encountered are given in brackets. An authoritative and fascinating book on this subject is *Star Names: Their Lore and Meaning* by R. H. Allen.

Explanatory Notes to the Constellation Maps

The hypothetical constellation CONSTEL appears as a pictorial key to the maps of the individual constellations.

CON . . . abbreviation of the name of the constellation
- red ground for constellations of the northern hemisphere
- yellow ground for constellations of the southern hemisphere
- black ground for equatorial constellations

CONSTEL . . . the Latin (international) name of the constellation

ABC, DEF, GHI. . . neighbouring constellations

A, B . . . . . conspicuous stars in the immediate vicinity

1 : scale of apparent stellar magnitude — the degrees of the scale (star discs) correspond to 0.5 magnitude.
2 : method of star designation. Next to each disc is written the name of the star. Most of the stars are marked with Greek letters or with Flamsteed's numbers. In the case of selected stars their distance in light years is also given. Colour differentiation of stars according to their distance:
   white . . . up to 100 light years
   orange . . . from 100 to 1000 light years
   red . . . more than 1000 light years
3 : double star with each of the two components visible with the naked eye or with opera glasses
4 : variable star — the outer circle denotes the maximum brightness and the inner the minimum brightness.
5 : variable star with a minimum of less than 5.3 magnitude
6 : open star cluster
7 : galactic nebula
8 : planetary nebula
9 : globular star cluster
10 : galaxy

White mark: the object is visible with the naked eye or with opera glasses.

Black mark: the object is visible only with a larger telescope.

Position of the maps: the longer arm (N) of the cross points to the north celestial pole.

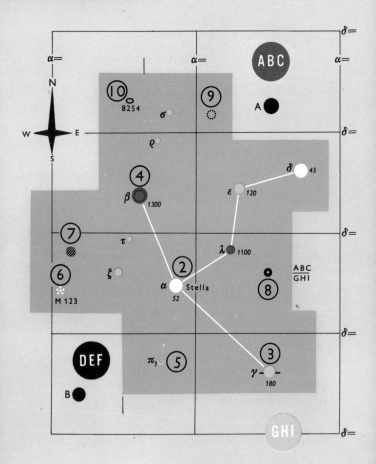

CON

① •5 •4 ●3 ●2 ⬤1

N
W ✦ E
S

ABC

⑩ 8254
σ
⑨
A ●

ρ

④ β 1300

δ 45
ε 120

⑦

τ

λ 1100

⑥ M 123

ξ

② α Stella 52

ABC GHI

⑧

DEF

π₁ ⑤

③ γ — 180

B ●

GHI

CONSTEL

ANDROMEDA
Andromedae   And   Andromeda

A prominent part of Andromeda contains a trio of stars with poetic names of Arabic origin. Sirrah represents the head of a chained woman, Mirach her hips, and Alamak her chained foot. These stars are associated with the ancient myth about the beautiful Andromeda who was to be sacrificed to a sea monster.

α **Andromedae,** or **Sirrah,** is a star with an apparent magnitude of 2.15. Its spectrum B8 is typical of helium stars, which have a temperature of 20,000°K. It is 105 light years distant and its absolute magnitude is −0.4.

β **Andromedae,** or **Mirach,** lies at a distance of 82 light years and its brightness is that of a star of magnitude 2.37. In reality it is a red giant of the spectral group MO with a relatively low temperature of about 3500°K. The absolute magnitude is 0.4.

γ **Andromedae,** or **Alamak,** is a double star with a colour contrast of orange and blue. The primary has a magnitude of 2.28, the companion a magnitude of 5.08. The separation of the two components is 10.0 seconds of arc, at present, so that a small telescope is needed to resolve them. The primary is a giant of the spectral group K2; its companion belongs to spectral group A0. This star lies at a distance of 160 light years.

NGC 224, or **M 31,** is the designation for the **Great Nebula,** a large spiral galaxy about 2,300,000 light years distant. Nebulae **NGC 225** and **M 32** (NGC 221) belong to the Andromeda system and can be likened to the Clouds of Magellan in the Milky Way. The Great Nebula can be seen with the unaided eye.

NGC 891 is a galaxy with a dark band of light-absorbing matter along its longitudinal axis. This nebula is positioned edgewise to the Earth.

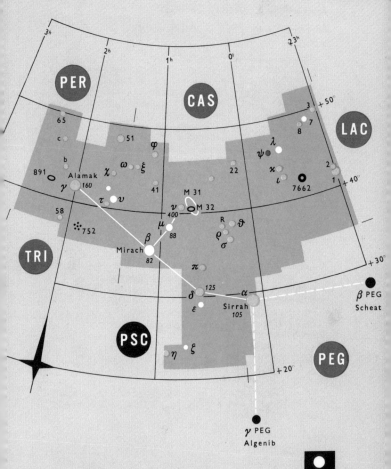

PER

CAS

LAC

TRI

PSC

PEG

3ʰ
2ʰ
1ʰ
0ʰ
23ʰ

+50°

+40°

+30°

+20°

65

c

b

891

γ
Alamak
160

58

752

51

φ

χ
ω
ξ

41

τ
υ

μ
88

β
Mirach
82

π

δ
ε
125

3
7
8

λ
ψ
x
ι
2
1
7662

22

ν
400

M 31

M 32

R
ϑ
ρ
σ

α
Sirrah
105

β PEG
Scheat

γ PEG
Algenib

η
ξ

ANDROMEDA

2
3
4
5

ANTLIA
Antliae   Ant   The Air Pump

The name Abbé de La Caille is one frequently encountered in connection with certain constellations of the southern sky. In his *Coelum Australe Stelliferum* of 1763, we encounter the strange name 'Air Pump', which undoubtedly memorializes Robert Boyle's *Machina Pneumatica* (as it was called on the Continent), which was a development from Otto von Guericke's inefficient single-piston air-pump. In the mid-eighteenth century de La Caille visited the southern hemisphere, and after his systematic survey of the sky in the region, he added some new constellations. The region is rather poor in stars compared with the northern hemisphere, and that is why the Air Pump has so few bright stars; it contains a small number of stars of barely 4th magnitude.

α **Antliae** is a star of 4.42 magnitude lying at a distance of 325 light years from the Earth. It belongs to the spectral group M0 comprising stars with a surface temperature much lower than that of the Sun, i.e. approximately 3500°K. The absolute magnitude is −0.6.

ε **Antliae** is a star of the same spectral type as the foregoing but lies at a distance of 400 light years. Its stellar magnitude is 4.64. If it were 32.6 light years distant, it would be brighter than Achernar of Eridanus.

ι **Antliae** belongs to the group of yellow stars because its spectrum G5 is similar to that of the Sun. It is 230 light years distant. The apparent magnitude is 4.70; the absolute magnitude is 0.4.

NGC 3132 is a planetary nebula which can be observed with a small telescope. It lies at an estimated distance of 1300 light years.

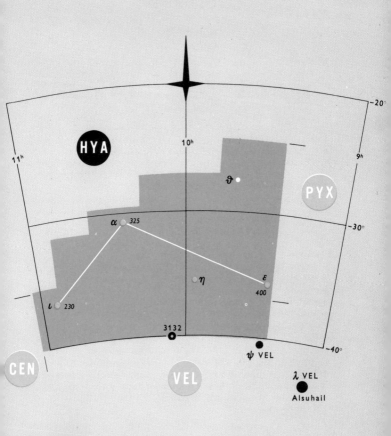

ANTLIA

HYA

PYX

ϑ

α 325

η

ε 400

ι 230

3132

ψ VEL

λ VEL
Alsuhail

CEN

VEL

10ʰ

11ʰ

9ʰ

−20°

−30°

−40°

2
3
4
5

APUS

Apodis   Aps   The Bird of Paradise

In Bayer's *Uranometria* of 1603, depicted among the constellations of the southern hemisphere is Apus Indica (Bird of Paradise). The original name of 'Apus' meant 'legless' and was mistakenly applied. The Greater Bird of Paradise, known in India, had a magnificent white, yellow and red plumage but unsightly legs, which were cut off by the natives desiring to offer the white man only the attractive part of the bird. The scientific name 'Apus' is now applied to swifts, and this name for the constellation is quite inappropriate. It is not a prominent constellation; it contains only a small number of stars, and is located near the south celestial pole above Triangulum Australe (The Southern Triangle).

α **Apodis** is the brightest star of the group; at a distance of 230 light years, it appears to the terrestrial observer as a star of magnitude 3.81. If it were 32.6 light years (10 parsecs) distant it would be almost as bright as Capella in the Charioteer. The spectrum of α Aps belongs to the group K5. These stars have a temperature lower than that of the Sun.

β **Apodis** belongs physically to those stars whose spectrum is somewhat like that of our Sun. Its brightness is that of a star of magnitude 4.16. At a distance of 10 parsecs however, it would have the luminosity of a star of magnitude 1.5. Its actual distance from the Earth is 109 light years.

γ **Apodis** is a sub-giant of the spectral class K0 which, lying at a distance of 105 light years, has the brightness of a star of magnitude 3.90. The absolute magnitude is 1.4.

$δ_1 δ_2$ **Apodis** is a fine double star of magnitudes 4.78 and 5.22. Both components belong to the same spectral group (the spectra are M5 and M1) comprising stars with a relatively low surface temperature of about 3500°K. The distance is 220 light years.

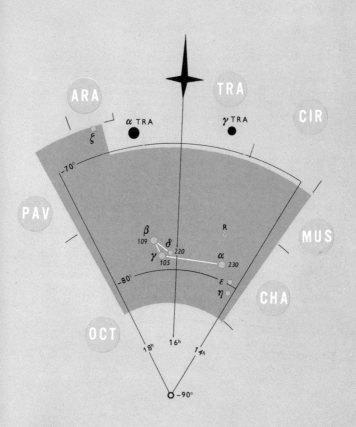

APUS

AQUARIUS

Aquarii   Aqr   The Water Carrier

The Water Carrier is a constellation rising above the southern horizon on autumn evenings. The stars of this group are comparatively faint and it requires some effort and imagination to discern the figure of a man on his knees pouring water from an amphora.

α **Aquarii,** or **Sadalmelek,** from the Arabic for 'Fortunate One of the King'. Physically it belongs among the supergiants of type GI, this spectrum being very similar to that of the Sun. It lies at a distance of 1350 light years, and shines like a star of magnitude 3.19. The absolute brightness is −5.5.

β **Aquarii,** or **Sadalsud,** is known in Arab astrology as the 'star of fortune throughout the world', the name also applying to another star very nearby. The heliacal rising of the two stars was carefully watched for because it marked the beginning of the rainy season; their setting marked the end of the monsoons. Sadalsud is a supergiant of the G0 group. It lies at a distance of 1100 light years and its brightness equals that of a star of magnitude 3.07. At a distance of 10 parsecs it would be as bright as Rigel in Orion.

δ **Aquarii,** or **Skat,** meaning 'a place whence something falls'. Modern science states that Skat lies at a distance of 78 light years and that its spectrum is A2, the type known as hydrogen stars. Its apparent magnitude is 3.51, the absolute magnitude 1.6.

ε **Aquarii,** or **Albali**, is a star of the spectral class A1, lying at a distance of 172 light years, with the brightness of a star of magnitude 3.83. The absolute magnitude is 0,2.

M 2, or **NGC 7089,** is a beautiful globular star cluster of the 7th magnitude.

Aquarius also contains the well-known and interesting planetary nebulae **NGC 7293,** known as **Hellix,** and **NGC 7009,** called **Saturn** because of its resemblance to that planet, caused by a dark band down the centre of the longitudinal axis of the nebula positioned edgewise to the Earth.

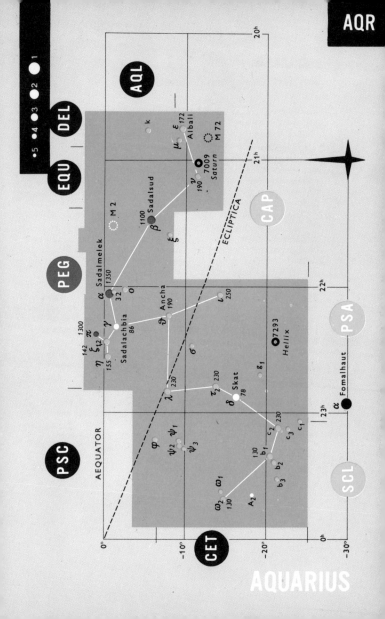

AQUILA

Aquilae   Aql   The Eagle

The Eagle is a small but beautiful constellation located in the Milky Way below Cygnus (the Swan). Altair, the prominent star of this constellation, cannot be missed.

α **Aquilae,** or **Altair,** from the Arabic *el nesr el-tair* meaning 'flying eagle', symbol of the ruler of Olympus. Today we know that it is a white star, spectral type A7, which is relatively close — only 16 light years from the Earth. Altair has an apparent magnitude of 0.89, and an absolute magnitude of 2.4.

β **Aquilae,** or **Alshain.** The meaning of this name is not known; in Sufi's day the stars α, β and γ were all known under the same name — Altair, flying eagle. Alshain, 42 light years distant, has an apparent brightness of 3.90. It is a yellow dwarf type G8, resembling our Sun both in size and physical properties. The absolute brightness is 3.3.

γ **Aquilae,** or **Reda,** or **Tarazed.** The name is of unknown origin and meaning. The star lies at a distance of 230 light years, and is seen by a terresterial observer as a star of magnitude 2.80. Its spectrum is type K3 and the surface temperature is approximately 4500°K. The absolute magnitude is -1.5.

δ **Aquilae,** or **Deneb Okab,** 'tail of the eagle', is a dwarf star of spectral type A5, which at a distance of 55 light years has the brightness of a star of magnitude 3.44. The absolute brightness is 2.3.

η **Aquilae** is the brightest cepheid-type variable with a period of 7.18 days, varying in brightness between the maximum of 4.1 and the minimum of 5.3. It is a giant star of the spectral group G0 and is 910 light years distant.

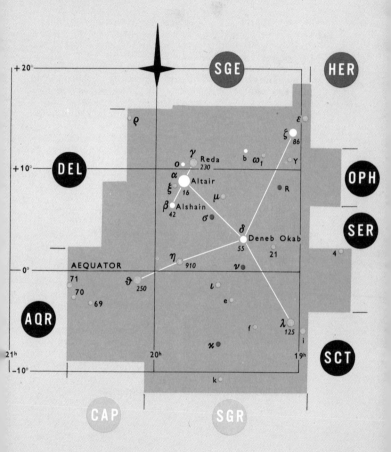

•5 ●4 ●3 ⬤2 ⬤1

SGE HER

ε
ξ
86

ϱ

Y

DEL

γ
o Reda
230
α
ξ
16
β
Alshain
42

Altair

b ω₁

μ

OPH

R

σ

δ
Deneb Okab
55

SER

η
910

21

4

AEQUATOR

71
70
69

ϑ
250

ν

ι

e

f

λ
125

i

AQR

x

k

21h

20h

19h

SCT

CAP SGR

AQUILA

ARA
Arae   Ara   The Altar

The constellation Ara was known to Greek and Roman astronomers. It was depicted on maps as a sacrificial altar named Thytérion by Áratos of Soli. Cicero adopted this term, giving it the Latin name Ara. Ara lies below the bend of the poisonous sting of Scorpius and comprises a number of stars of which only the brightest are listed below.

α **Arae,** spectral type B3, lies at a distance of 220 light years. On the Earth's horizon it shines like a star of magnitude 2.97. At a distance of 10 parsecs it would be as bright as one of the major stars of Gemini.

β **Arae** is a star of magnitude 2.80 lying at a distance of 930 light years. Its spectrum belongs to class K1. Absolute brightness −0.5.

γ **Arae** is a helium star. It lies at a distance of 1020 light years and has an apparent brightness of magnitude 3.51. Its absolute magnitude is −4.3.

δ **Arae,** 148 light years away, has an apparent magnitude of 3.79, spectral class B8, and effective temperature approximately 20,000°K. Absolute magnitude 0.5.

ζ **Arae** is a star of magnitude 3.06 and spectral class K5, with effective temperature of approximately 4500°K. Light from this star takes 155 years to reach Earth. The absolute magnitude is −0.3.

η **Arae** is an orange star, spectral type K5, lying at a distance of 163 light years. The apparent visual magnitude is 3.68, the absolute magnitude 0.2.

ϑ **Arae,** 1600 light years distant, appears to a terrestrial observer as a star of magnitude 3.90. Absolute magnitude is −5.2.

NGC 6397 is a planetary nebula which can be discerned with a small telescope as a hazy disc.

NGC 6193 is a bright, open star cluster.

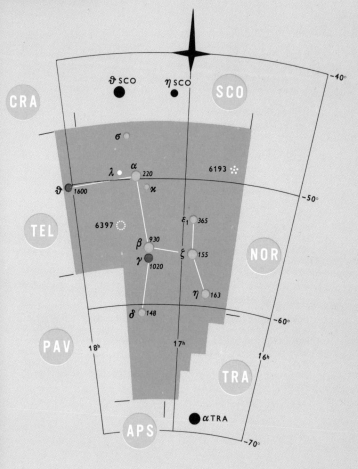

ARA

●5 ●4 ●3 ○2

ARA

CRA

ϑ SCO   η SCO   SCO

σ

λ   α
          220   6193
ϑ 1600   ϰ

TEL   6397   ε₁ 365

β 930   ξ 155   NOR
γ 1020

η 163

δ 148   -60°

PAV   18ʰ   17ʰ   16ʰ   TRA

APS   α TRA

-70°

ARA

ARIES

Arietis   Ari   The Ram

The constellation Aries, the first sign of the zodiac, was once of great importance for the calendar. It has retained its place of honour even though precession has caused the vernal point to shift into Pisces. The Ram is also associated with the legend of the Argonaut expedition in quest of the Golden Fleece. As a constellation the Ram is an inconspicuous group of three brighter stars lying between Pisces on the east and Taurus on the west.

α **Arietis,** or **Hamal,** originally the Arabic name for the whole constellation as well as for this one star. Today we know that α Arietis is a giant star lying at a distance of 78 light years; it appears to be a star of magnitude 2.23. At a distance of 10 parsecs its brightness would be of the order of 0.3. The star's spectrum is K2, the metallic lines being the most intense. The surface temperature is 4500°K.

β **Arietis,** or **Sheratan,** from the Arabic *al Sharat*, meaning 'mark' or 'sign'. Its spectrum ranks this star in the group of hydrogen stars with the comparatively high temperature of approximately 10,000°K. The apparent visual magnitude is 2.72, the absolute magnitude 1.8. The distance from the Earth is about 50 light years.

$\gamma_1\gamma_2$ **Arietis,** or **Mesarthim,** translated somewhat uncertainly as 'two marks', perhaps from the fact that Mesarthim is a fine optical double star. It was determined as such by the English observer Robert Hooke as early as 1664. Both components are of about equal brightness (4.83—4.75) and the spectrum, A0 in both stars, showing them to be hydrogen stars. The first and the brighter of the two stars is 148 light years distant, the second 172 light years. The duality is caused by the accidental effect of perspective, the two stars lying near to the same line of sight from the observer.

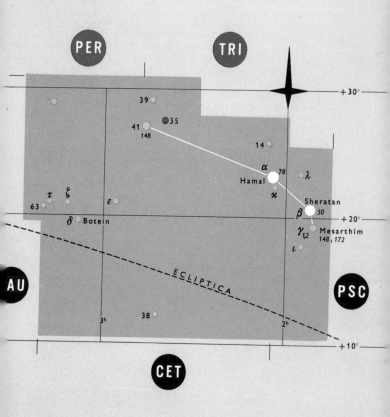

ARI

PER   TRI

●5 ●4 ●3 ◯2

+30°

39

35

41
148

14

α   78
Hamal

λ

κ

Sheratan

τ ξ

63

δ Botein

ε

β   50

+20°

γ₁,₂
148, 172

Mesarthim

ι

AU

ECLIPTICA

PSC

3ʰ

38

2ʰ

+10°

CET

ARIES

AURIGA

Aurigae   Aur   The Charioteer

The original Greek name for this constellation was Heniochos, 'one who holds the reins', in other words, 'charioteer'. Auriga (charioteer) is the Latin name. It is a very large constellation with Capella as the chief star. According to Apollodorus, Capella is the nymph Amalthea whom Jupiter rewarded by placing her among the stars.

α **Aurigae,** or **Capella,** 'little she-goat', is a giant star of spectral class G5 and G0, which shows that it is a spectroscopic binary with an invisible companion. Both stars belong to the same spectral group as the Sun. Capella lies at a distance of only 45 light years and appears as a star of magnitude 0.21. At 10 parsecs its brightness would increase to −0.6.

β **Aurigae,** or **Menkalinan,** from the Arabic for 'shoulder of the charioteer'. It is a variable star with a barely discernible amplitude of magnitude 1.9 to 2.0. The spectrum is that of the hydrogen stars, namely A2. It is 65 light years distant.

ε **Aurigae** is a well-known variable of the Algol type whose brightness varies in a period of 9883 days between the maximum of 3.4 and minimum of 4.5. This star is a supergiant of the spectral class F0 lying at a distance of 3300 light years.

ϑ **Aurigae** is 116 light years distant and has an apparent magnitude of 2.71. The spectrum is A0, of the hydrogen stars, and the surface temperature approximately 10,000°K. The absolute magnitude is 0.0.

The Charioteer contains a number of open star clusters: **M 36** (NGC 1960), **M 37** (NGC 2097), **M 38** (NGC 5236), **NGC 2281** and **NGC 1907.**

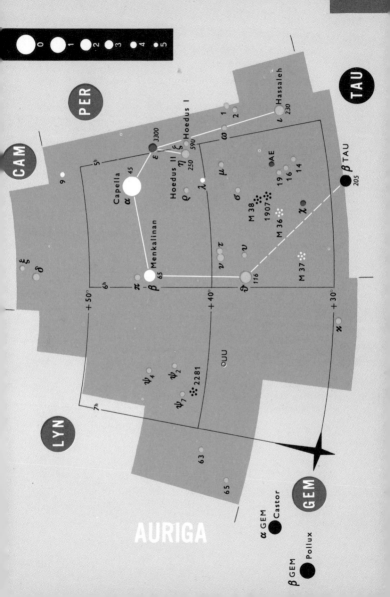

PER

CAM

TAU

LYN

GEM

AURIGA

9

Hassaleh
ι
230

Hoedus I
ζ
590

ε
3300

Hoedus II
η
250

Capella
α
45

ω

1

2

μ

λ

ρ

AE

19

16

14

M 38

1907

M 36

χ

β TAU
205

σ

Menkalinan
β
65

τ

ν

υ

ϑ
116

M 37

π

κ

ξ
δ

ψ₄

ψ₂

2281

ψ₇

63

65

α GEM
Castor

β GEM
Pollux

+ 50°

+ 40°

+ 30°

5ʰ

6ʰ

7ʰ

0 1 2 3 4 5

BOÖTES
Boötis   Boo   The Herdsman

Boötes is notable for its bright star Arcturus. The most important stars of this constellation are as follows:

α **Boötis,** or **Arcturus,** from the Greek for 'bearkeeper', is a giant star of spectral class K2. Its diameter is almost 23 times larger than that of the Sun. It is a relatively close star, being only 35 light years distant. The apparent magnitude is 0.24; the absolute magnitude is −0.1.

β **Boötis,** or **Nekkar,** from the Arabic *el nakkar*, the meaning of which is uncertain, is a giant of the spectral group G5; its apparent magnitude is 3.63, the absolute magnitude 0.5. This star lies at a distance of 136 light years.

γ **Boötis** was called **Haris** by the Arabs, meaning 'sentinel of the north'. It is a dwarf star with spectrum A7, apparent magnitude 3.00, and absolute magnitude 0.6, lying at a distance of 99 light years.

δ **Boötis** is a yellow giant of spectral class G4, 116 light years distant. Its brightness is of magnitude 3.54. The absolute magnitude is 0.8.

ε **Boötis,** or **Izar,** Arabic for 'girdle', is a yellow giant of spectral class K0. It is a triple star system. The existence of one of these stars is revealed in the spectrum of Izar. The visual magnitude of the primary is 2.70; the absolute magnitude is −1.6. The system is 230 light years distant. The visual binary is so lovely when observed with a larger telescope that it has been dubbed **Pulcherrima** (most beautiful).

Boötes contains a number of other double stars. Those which have a component of at least 5th visual magnitude are: μ **Boötis,** π **Boo,** ζ **Boo.**

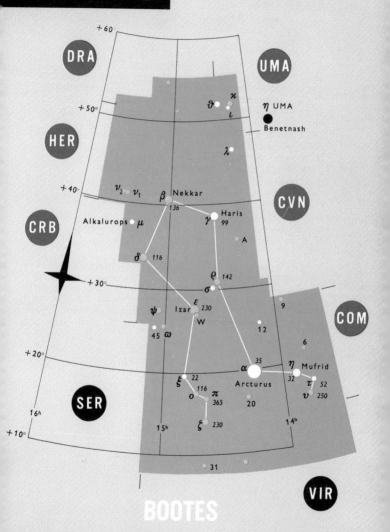

•5 •4 ●3 ●2 ●1 ⬤0

DRA

UMA

HER

ϑ х
ι

η UMA
Benetnash

λ

CVN

ν₂ ν₁   β Nekkar
              136

Alkalurops ○ μ

γ Haris
    99

CRB

δ 116

A

ρ 142
σ

+30°

ψ   ε 230
   Izar
      W

+20°

ψ
45 ○ ω

ξ 22
      116
  ο π
      365
    ξ 230

α 35

Arcturus

9

12

6

η Mufrid
32

τ 52
υ 250

20

COM

SER

16ʰ

15ʰ

14ʰ

+10°

31

VIR

BOOTES

CAELUM
Caeli   Cae   The Graving Tool

In 1763 Nicolas Louis de La Caille published *Coelum Australe Stelliferum*, in which he gave odd names to certain amorphous areas amidst the stars. One of these is Caelum. The four feeble stars forming the backbone of this constellation could just as easily have been incorporated in Eridanus or Columba. However, they were assigned to Caelum and have remained so to this day.

α **Caeli** is a yellowish star with spectrum F1 and temperature somewhat higher than that of the Sun. Its brightness is of magnitude 4.52; the absolute magnitude is 2.8. Light from this star takes 72 years to reach the Earth.

β **Caeli** lies somewhat closer, 69 light years. It is a star of magnitude 5.08 and spectral group F0. The absolute brightness is 3.7.

γ **Caeli** is an orange star because the spectrum is most intense around the line K5. Its magnitude is 4.62 and it lies at a distance of 230 light years. The absolute magnitude is 0.3.

δ **Caeli** is a star of apparent visual magnitude 5.16. Nothing more is known to date other than that it belongs to the spectral class B3 characterized by neutral helium absorption bands, hence the name helium stars. The surface temperature of this type of star is approximately 20,000°K. δ Caeli is travelling away from the Earth at a speed of 15 km/sec.

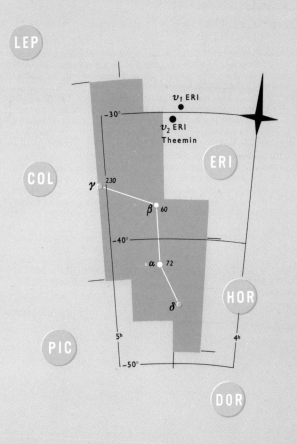

CAE

LEP

v_1 ERI

v_2 ERI
Theemin

ERI

COL

γ 230

β 60

−30°

−40°

α 72

δ

HOR

5ʰ

4ʰ

PIC

−50°

DOR

CAELUM

• 4
• 5

CAMELOPARDALIS

Camelopardalis   Cam   The Giraffe

Between Auriga and Polaris there is a region almost devoid of stars. Few are of such magnitude as would attract one's attention and prompt one to group them into some sort of system. In 1624 Jacob Bartsch conceived the name Camelopardalis for this region (in his work *Usus Astronomicus Planisphaerium Argentinae*). As astronomers dislike changing the names of established constellations, it has remained the Giraffe to this day. Of the whole group only the following two stars are clearly discernible with the naked eye.

α **Camelopardalis,** 3300 light years distant, appears as an unusually bright star. This is borne out by its spectrum 09. The effective temperature is 35,000°K. Stars such as this are very rare. The apparent magnitude of α Camelopardalis is 4.38. If it were 10 parsecs distant, its brightness would be that of a star of magnitude −6.3, brighter than any star in the sky.

β **Camelopardalis** is a super-giant of the spectral class G2, which to the terrestrial observer appears as a star of a magnitude of barely 4.22. However, if it were 10 parsecs distant it would glow brightly in the heavens like a star of magnitude −5.2. It lies at a distance of 1700 light years.

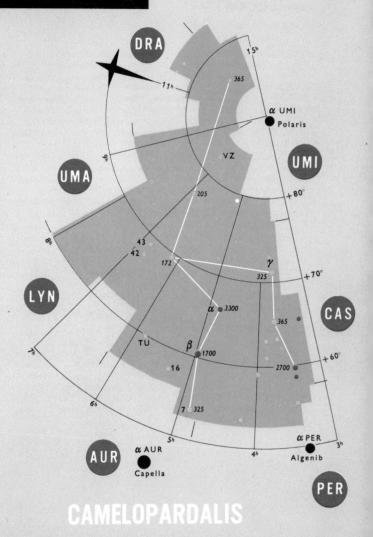

DRA

UMA

UMI

LYN

CAS

AUR

PER

α UMI
Polaris

365

VZ

205

43
42
172

γ
325

α 3300

365

TU

β
1700

16

2700

7 325

α PER
Algenib

α AUR
Capella

+80°

+70°

+60°

15h

11h

9h

8h

7h

6h

5h

4h

3h

•5 •4 •3 •2 •1 •0

CAMELOPARDALIS

CANCER
Cancri Cnc The Crab

An inconspicuous constellation comprising stars of less than 4th magnitude. The names of these stars are rather odd: one is called Acubens, meaning 'claws'; the other two are Asellus Borealis and Asellus Australis — 'northern donkey' and 'southern donkey'. Perhaps this has some connection with the open star cluster M 44 lying in their midst and known as the Manger. According to the Greek version, the donkeys were put in the heavens by Olympus to encourage the gods with their braying in the latter's fight with the giants.

α **Cancri,** or **Acubens,** is a double star lying at a distance of 99 light years. The primary has a visual magnitude of 4.27; the other component is of 11th magnitude. Because they have a separation of only 11 seconds of arc at present, a telescope is necessary for their resolution. The primary belongs to spectral class F0.

γ **Cancri,** or **Asellus Borealis.** This star of magnitude 4,73 would have the same luminosity as Asellus Australis if it were 32.6 light years distant. However, it lies at a distance of 230 light years.

δ **Cancri,** or **Asellus Australis,** appears to be a faint star of magnitude 4.17. In reality, however, it is a giant of spectral class K0. The absolute magnitude is 0.0 which means that if it were 10 parsecs distant it would appear as bright to the terrestrial observer as Vega in Lyra. It lies at a distance of 220 light years.

ζ **Cancri** is a double star first observed by Tobias Mayer. The brighter component has a magnitude of 5.1, the second a magnitude of 6.0. The two have a separation of 5.9 seconds and can be observed with a small telescope. A third component was first observed on 21 November 1781 by William Herschel; it lies in the immediate vicinity of the primary. In actual fact then this is a system of three stars lying at a distance of 78 light years.

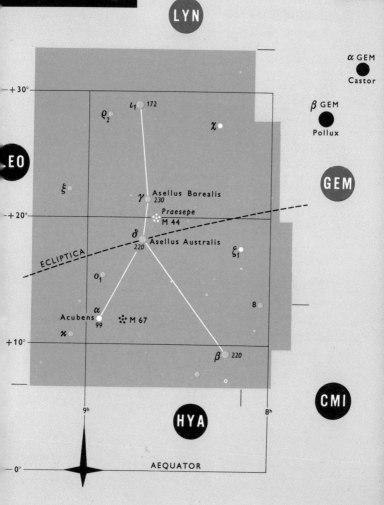

CNC

●5 ●4 ●3 ●2 ●1

LYN

α GEM
Castor

β GEM
Pollux

+30°

ρ₂   ι₁ ○ 172

χ ●

EO

ξ ●

GEM

γ ○ Asellus Borealis
230

+20°
Praesepe
M 44

δ ○ Asellus Australis
220

ECLIPTICA

ξ₁ ●

o₁ ●

α
Acubens ○   ∴ M 67
99

8 ●

κ ●

+10°

β ○ 220

9ʰ

HYA

8ʰ

CMI

0°

AEQUATOR

CANCER

CANES VENATICI
Canum Venaticorum   CVn   The Hunting Dogs

This amorphous constellation was named by the astronomer J. Hevelius. In 1690, in his *Prodromus Astronomiae*, he assigned to it several faint stars below Ursa Major without any inkling that here were large clusters of distant galaxies extending into Coma Berenices. In old maps the Hunting Dogs were depicted as a pair of dogs.

α **Canum Venaticorum** is called **Cor Caroli,** meaning 'Charles' Heart'. It is a double star of magnitudes 2.80 and 5.39, lying at a distance of 130 light years. The absolute brightness of the first component is −0.1 and that of the second is 2.4. The spectra are identical − A0, the hydrogen stars. The temperature is high, approximately 10,000°K. These stars are white.

β **Canum Venaticorum,** or **Asterion,** is a dwarf of spectral class G0. The apparent visual magnitude is 4.32 and the absolute magnitude is 4.5. It is 30 light years distant.

γ **Canum Venaticorum** is a variable star with semi-regular period during which the magnitude changes from 5.2 to 6.6. It is not visible to the naked eye but can be viewed with opera glasses. This star belongs to the spectral group N3 where the continuous spectrum ends, only the long waves remaining. That is why stars of this type are an intense red.

As has already been stated the Hunting Dogs contain many distant galaxies of various shape and size. These, however, are objects better suited for photography with a large telescope. One of them is the spiral nebula **M 51** which has the brightness of a star of the 10th magnitude and is visible with a medium telescope.

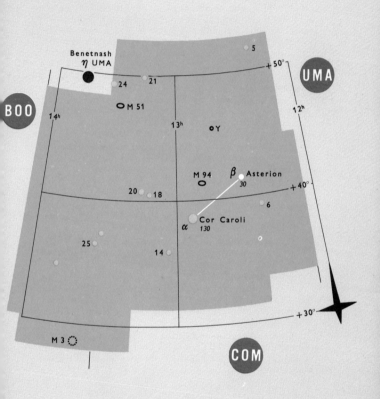

•5 •4 •3 ◯2

UMA

BOO

14ʰ

Benetnash
η UMA

24   21

◯ M 51

13ʰ

+50°

12ʰ

5

•Y

M 94   β ◦ Asterion
◯   30

20 ◦18

α ◦ Cor Caroli
130

25

14

6

+40°

+30°

M 3 ◌

COM

CANES VENATICI

CANIS MAJOR

Canis Majoris   CMa   The Greater Dog

α **Canis Majoris,** or **Sirius,** from the Greek for 'scorching', is 9 light years distant. Its magnitude is -1.37 and its diameter is double that of the Sun. It belongs to spectral class A1. Of greater interest to astronomers is the star's companion **Sirius B.** It is a white dwarf and has a density more than 90,000 times greater than that of the Sun. Sirius B revolves about the primary once in 50 years. One of the best times for observation will be in 1973.

β **Canis Majoris,** or **Mirzam,** from the Arabic *al murzim* meaning the 'announcer'. Its distance is 650 light years and its magnitude is 1.99. At a distance of 10 parsecs it would be many times brighter than Sirius A.

γ **Canis Majoris,** or **Muliphein,** a name probably of Arabic origin, is a star of magnitude 4.07. Its distance is 325 light years and its absolute magnitude is -0.9. It belongs to spectral class B8.

δ **Canis Majoris,** or **Wezen,** from the Arabic *al wazn* meaning 'weight', lies at a distance of 1100 light years and belongs to spectral class G3. It has an apparent magnitude of 1.98; the absolute brightness is -5.9.

ε **Canis Majoris,** or **Adara,** from the Arabic for 'virgins', is a super-giant with the B1 spectrum of helium stars. At its distance of 470 light years its brightness is of magnitude 1.63. The absolute brightness is -4.4.

ζ **Canis Majoris,** or **Furud,** probably from the Arabic for 'bright single ones', lies at a distance of 250 light years. Its apparent magnitude is 3.1. Spectral group B5. Absolute magnitude -1.3.

η **Canis Majoris,** or **Aludra,** uncertain meaning, is a star of magnitude 2.43 lying at a distance of 1300 light years. In reality it is a super-giant of spectral class B5. Absolute magnitude -6.0.

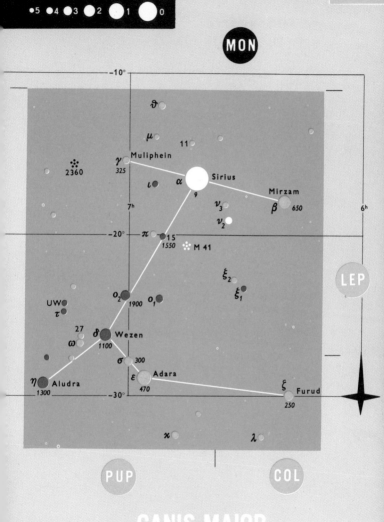

MON

2360

θ

μ

11

γ Muliphein
325

ι

α Sirius
9

Mirzam
β 650

ν₃

ν₂

7ʰ

6ʰ

π

15
1550

M 41

ξ₂

ξ₁

UW
τ

o₂
1900

o₁

27

ω

δ Wezen
1100

σ 300

Adara

η Aludra
1300

ε
470

ξ Furud
250

κ

λ

PUP

COL

LEP

CANIS MAIOR

CANIS MAJOR

CANIS MINOR

Canis Minoris   CMi   The Lesser Dog

There are several legends associated with the Lesser Dog. Eratosthenes saw him as Orion's companion; Hyginus called him Maera, the dog mourning the death of his master Icarus. The morning rising of this constellation in Rome fell on July 15, at the hottest time of the year. Because it preceded the rising of Canis Major with Sirius on the tip of its nose it was called Pro Tu Kynos by the Greeks, meaning 'before the Great Dog', hence the name Procyon. The Arabic name Al Kalb Al Mutakaddim meant 'the preceding dog', but did not become established in astronomical terminology.

α **Canis Minoris,** or **Procyon,** belongs to the group of stars that lies in relatively close proximity to the Sun, being only 11 light years distant from the Earth. It is a sub-giant of spectral class F5 and has an apparent brightness of 0.48. The absolute magnitude is 2.7. Like Sirius, Procyon also has a white dwarf companion, i.e. a star of unusually great density. Its diameter is a mere one-hundredth of the Sun's, but its weight is 63 percent of the Sun's. The companion is of the 9th magnitude and is 4.3 seconds distant from the primary component. The two revolve round a common centre of gravity once every 40 years.

β **Canis Minoris,** or **Gomeisa,** possibly from *al ghumaisa*, 'the weeping one', is a star of 3.09 stellar magnitude, absolute brightness 0.0 and spectral type B8. It is 136 light years distant.

γ **Canis Minoris,** lying at a distance of 250 light years, has an apparent magnitude of 4.60. In fact it is a yellow giant K4. The absolute magnitude is 0.2.

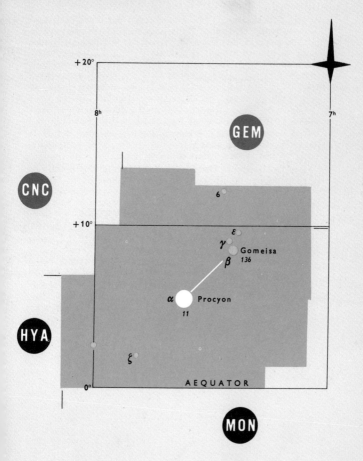

CMI

●5 ●4 ●3 ●2 ●1 ○0

+20°

8h

7h

GEM

CNC

6

+10°

ε

γ

Gomeisa

β

136

α

Procyon

11

HYA

ξ

AEQUATOR

0°

MON

CANIS MINOR

CAPRICORNUS
Capricorni   Cap   The Goat

At the end of August one can observe the constellation of Capricorn, the tenth sign of the zodiac. A straight line drawn from the bright star Vega in Lyra through Altair in Aquila leads to the four stars α_1 and α_2, β and γ of Capricorn, marking the horns of the satyr.

α **Capricorni,** or **Gredi** (Giedi), Arabic for the animal Ibex, comprises two stars which, because of their apparently close proximity, may be said to be a double. In reality $\alpha\,1$ is 1100 light years away, whereas $\alpha\,2$ is only 116 light years away. The two stars have similar spectra, namely G5 and G8; however the first is a super-giant and the second merely a giant. α_1 has a magnitude of 4.55; α_2 is somewhat brighter with a magnitude of 3.77.

β **Capricorni,** or **Dabih,** from the Arabic for 'lucky one of the slaughterers', is a dwarf of the spectral group F8 and B8. The apparent magnitude is 3.25; the absolute brightness is -1.2. It lies at a distance of 250 light years.

δ **Capricorni,** or **Deneb Algiedi** (Deneb Algedi), meaning 'goat's tail', has an A5 spectrum and is a variable star of the Algol type. The light varies by a bare 0.2 stellar magnitude. The changes are caused by its companion, whose motion is revealed in the spectrum of the primary. It is 50 light years distant and has a brightness of 2.98.

ε **Capricorni,** though it has an apparent brightness of only 3.86, is a super-giant of the spectral group G4, lying at a distance of 470 light years. The absolute magnitude is -2.2.

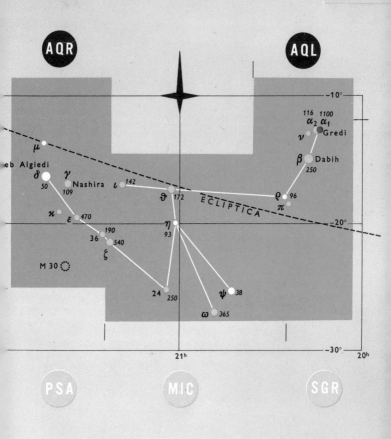

AQR

AQL

-10°

116 1100
α₂ α₁
ν   Gredi

β   Dabih
250

eb Algiedi
δ
50

γ
Nashira
109

ι 142

ϑ 172

ϱ   96
π

ECLIPTICA

μ

ϰ

ε 470

36

190

ξ 540

η
93

-20°

M 30

24 250

ψ 38

ω 365

21ʰ

-30°

20ʰ

PSA

MIC

SGR

CAPRICORNUS

3
4
5

CARINA
Carinae   Car   The Keel

The three constellations Carina, Puppis and Vela were once part of the constellation known as Argo Navis. The brightest star Canopus is found in Carina and frequently serves for the navigation of space vehicles.

α **Carinae,** or **Canopus,** the Latin version of the Greek Canobos, the name of the pilot of Menelaos' fleet, who on his return from the destruction of Troy died in Egypt, where a town also was named after him. The star Canopus, magnitude −0.86, is a super-giant of the spectral group F0 lying at a distance of 365 light years.

β **Carinae,** or **Miaplacidus,** the 'keel', is the second brightest of the hydrogen stars with spectrum A0. It is 105 light years distant and has an apparent magnitude of 1.80. The absolute magnitude is −0.9.

ε **Carinae** has an apparent magnitude of 1.74. The composite spectrum K0-B indicates that this is a spectroscopic binary lying at a distance of 325 light years. The absolute magnitude is −3.0.

ϑ **Carinae,** lying close to a group of faint stars, has an apparent magnitude of 3.03. It belongs to the group of helium stars B0 with an effective temperature of 20,000°K. It is 930 light years distant.

ι **Carinae,** or **Tureis** (Turais), from the Arabic for the stern ornament of an ancient ship, has an apparent brightness of 2.25. At a distance of 10 parsecs it would be as bright as Venus at its brightest. Its distance from the Earth is 1400 light years.

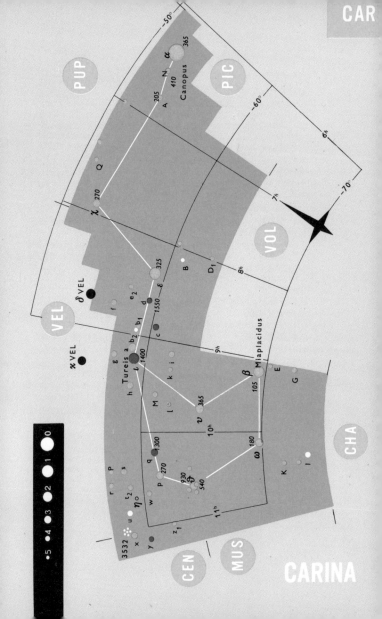

CASSIOPEIA

Cassiopeiae   Cas   Cassiopeia

Cassiopeia is a prominent constellation comprising a W-shaped group of five bright stars. Legend has it that Cassiopeia was the mother of Andromeda, who was supposed to have been sacrificed to the sea monster ravaging the land of the Ethiopian king Cepheus.

α **Cassiopeiae,** or **Schedir** (Schedar), is a giant of the spectral class K0 lying at a distance of 163 light years. At this distance the terrestrial observer sees it as a star of magnitude 2.47; the absolute magnitude is 0.1.

β **Cassiopeiae,** or **Caph,** is a dwarf, spectrum F2, 47 light years distant. The apparent brightness is 2.42, the absolute brightness 1.6.

γ **Cassiopeiae,** or **Cih,** is a giant star of spectral group B0. It is of interest to astronomers because of the change in luminosity from magnitude 1.6 to 3.0, caused probably by the varying diameter of its gaseous shell. Its distance is 650 light years.

δ **Cassiopeiae,** or **Rucbar,** or **Ksora,** 'knee', is a star of spectral class A3 lying at a distance of 76 light years. The absolute magnitude is 1.0.

ε **Cassiopeiae,** or **Segin,** lying at a distance of 470 light years, has an apparent magnitude of 3.34. The spectral group is B0, absolute brightness -2.3.

ϱ **Cassiopeiae** is an irregular-period variable ranging in brightness from magnitude 4.1 to 6.2. It is 830 light years distant.

This constellation includes several open star clusters — **M 52, M 103** and **NGC 457.**

In 1572 a supernova observed by Tycho Brahe appeared in Cassiopeia. It reached a maximum brightness of -4, which is greater than that of Venus. This was caused by a radical transformation of the stellar structure in the last phase of the star's evolution. The velocity of expansion of the gaseous shell must have been fantastic — an estimated 9000 kilometres per second. The estimated distance of the supernova is 11,400 light years.

124

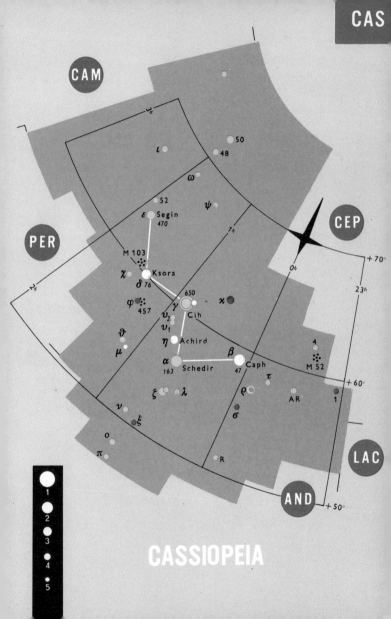

CENTAURUS

Centauri   Cen   The Centaur

Most of this constellation is visible above the horizon in the southern sky when the tail of Hydra is above Centaurus.

α **Centauri,** or **Toliman,** meaning 'grape-vine shoot', also called **Rigel Kentaurus,** 'foot of the centaur'. Both names relate to the original depiction of the centaur as part man and part horse, holding in his hand a staff encircled by a grape vine. α Centauri is a double star. One component has a spectrum like that of our Sun, namely G4. Together the two components have a brightness of the order of 0.06.

Proxima Centauri is mentioned here although it is of the 9th magnitude. It is a red dwarf K5, lying close to α Centauri. It is the star closest to our stellar system, being only 4.3 light years away.

β **Centauri,** or **Agena,** is a bright giant of spectral class B3, lying at a distance of 325 light years. It has a companion of the 9th magnitude, at present 1.2 seconds of arc distant from the primary. It is resolvable with a good telescope. The total brightness of Agena is 0.86, the absolute brightness −4.3.

γ **Centauri** is a hydrogen type star with approximate temperature of 10,000°K. The brightness is that of a 2.38 magnitude star lying at a distance of 130 light years.

δ **Centauri** is a helium star, spectral type B3, 220 light years distant from the Earth. The apparent magnitude is 2.88, the absolute magnitude −1.2.

Centaurus contains numerous interesting objects, as the Milky Way passes through it. The most remarkable is ω **Centauri,** a giant globular cluster visible to the unaided eye, lying at a distance of 5000 parsecs.

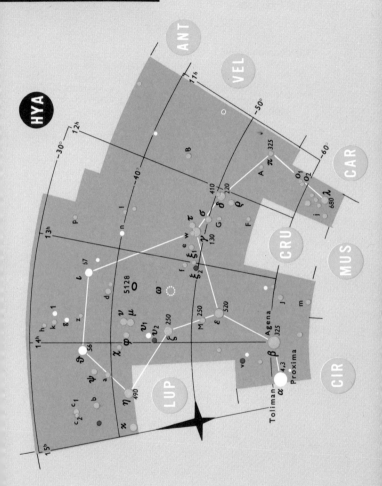

ANT

VEL

HYA

CAR

CRU

MUS

CIR

LUP

CENTAURUS

CEPHEUS
Cephei Cep Cepheus

Between Cassiopeia and Draco lies a figure marked by four bright stars which was given the name Cepheus. Part of the constellation is intersected by the Milky Way and is rich in small stars. According to Greek mythology, Cepheus was the king of Ethiopia and father of the beautiful Andromeda.

α **Cephei,** or **Alderamin,** meaning 'right shoulder', is a giant star of spectral group A7, lying at a distance of 49 light years. To the terrestrial observer it appears as a star of magnitude 2.60. The absolute brightness is 1.7.

β **Cephei,** or **Alfirk,** Arabic for 'herd', is in fact a double star. The primary star is a variable with small amplitude ranging between 3.30 and 3.35. Astronomers refer to it as a variable of the β Cephei type. Alfirk belongs to the class of giant stars. It is 740 light years distant from the Earth.

γ **Cephei,** or **Alrai** (Arrai), from the Arabic for 'shepherd'. This star is a sub-giant of spectral class K1 lying at a distance of 50 light years.

δ **Cephei** is a well-known type of variable of the class known as cepheids. Its brightness ranges between magnitudes 4.1 and 5.2 in a period of 5.37 days. At the maximum it is a super-giant of the spectral group F5, at the minimum of the spectral group G0. The diameter of the star when it is brightest is 35.4 times that of the Sun and 31.6 times the Sun's diameter when it is at the minimum. This star is 930 light years away.

The constellation Cepheus contains a great number of variable stars, double stars and star clusters.

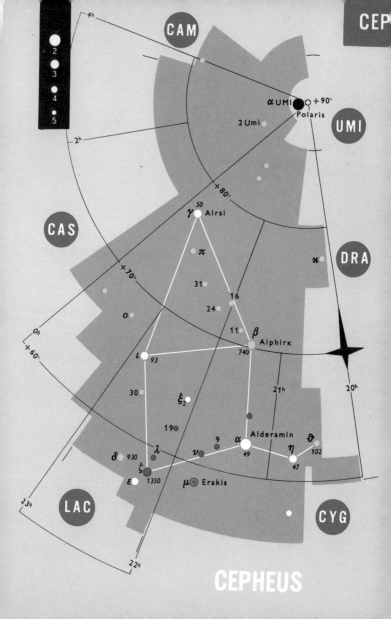

CETUS

Ceti   Cet   The Whale

α **Ceti,** or **Menkar,** meaning 'nose' according to former zoological concepts. This star is a red giant of the spectral class M2 lying at a distance of 130 light years. The apparent magnitude is 2.82, the absolute magnitude −0.2.

β **Ceti,** or **Deneb Kaitos,** from the Arabic for 'southern branch of the tail', is a giant of spectral group K0, 64 light years distant from the solar system. The visual magnitude is 2.24, the absolute magnitude 0.8.

γ **Ceti,** or **Kaffaljidhma,** has a composite spectrum A2-F7. Light from this star takes 82 years to reach the Earth. The absolute magnitude is 1.6, but a terrestrial observer sees it as a star of magnitude 3.58.

ζ **Ceti,** or **Baten Kaitos,** from the Arabic for 'whale's belly', is a giant of the spectral type K0 with apparent magnitude of 3.92 at a distance of 148 light years. The absolute magnitude is 0.6.

ϑ **Ceti** is a sub-giant of the spectral class K0, 112 light years distant. The apparent brightness is 3.83, the absolute brightness 1.1.

υ **Ceti** is a red giant, a colour corresponding to its spectrum M1. It is 230 light years distant and has an apparent magnitude of 4.18. At a distance of 10 parsecs it would shine as brightly as Aldebaran.

μ **Ceti** is a dwarf, 102 light years away, with an apparent magnitude of 4.36. The spectral group is F4 and the absolute brightness 1.9.

ο **Ceti,** or **Mira Ceti,** 'wonderful star', is a typical long-period variable star with amplitude ranging from magnitude 2.0 to 10.1. The star was first observed in 1596 by D. Fabricius. The period of luminosity variation is 331 days. Its distance from the Earth is 820 light years.

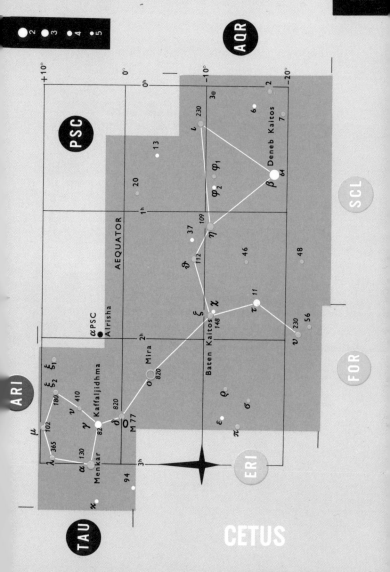

CET

AQR

PSC

SCL

FOR

ERI

TAU

ARI

CETUS

AEQUATOR

+10°   0°   -10°   -20°

0ʰ

1ʰ

2ʰ

3ʰ

● 2 ● 3 ● 4 • 5

ι 230

3

2

6

7

Deneb Kaitos

φ₁

φ₂

β 64

13

20

η 109

37

ϑ 112

46

48

χ

ξ 148

τ 11

56

Baten Kaitos

ν 230

α PSC
Alrisha

ο Mira
820

ρ

σ

ε

π

M 77

δ 820

ο

γ 82

Kaffaljidhma

ν 410

ξ₂ 180

ξ₁

μ

λ 365

102

α 130

Menkar

94

ϰ

CHAMAELEON

Chamaeleonis   Cha   The Chameleon

The name of this reptile has remained in use, unlike many other curiosities among the stars such as the Thrush, Cat, Reindeer, and other names introduced by observers of the southern sky, which have passed into oblivion. Chamaeleon lies above the bright star Miaplacidus in Carina, close to the south celestial pole. Its stars are faint, being between the 4th and 5th magnitude.

α **Chamaeleonis,** lying at a distance of 67 light years, appears to the terrestrial observer as a star of magnitude 4.08. The absolute magnitude is 2.5; the spectrum F5 is characteristic of yellowish stars with a temperature of 7500°K.

β **Chamaeleonis** is a helium star with the high temperature of approximately 20,000°K. It is 250 light years distant; the apparent magnitude is 4.38, the absolute magnitude 0.0.

γ **Chamaeleonis,** 820 light years distant, appears to the terrestrial observer as a star of magnitude 4.1. Its spectrum M0 is typical of red stars. The surface temperature is approximately 3500°K. If this star were 32.6 light years distant it would be as bright as Betelgeuse in Orion.

δ_2 **Chamaeleonis** is a star of spectral group B5 lying at a distance of 410 light years. It is the primary of an optical binary. The absolute magnitude is -0.9. It appears very close to δ_1 **Chamaeleonis,** 1088 light years distant from the Earth. This fact alone indicates that the two stars are only seemingly close. The spectral group is also different, namely K2. The temperature is lower than that of the Sun and therefore its colour is orange. The absolute magnitude is -2.1. Although its brightness is 5.48 and thus invisible to the unaided eye, nevertheless it is included here as a matter of interest.

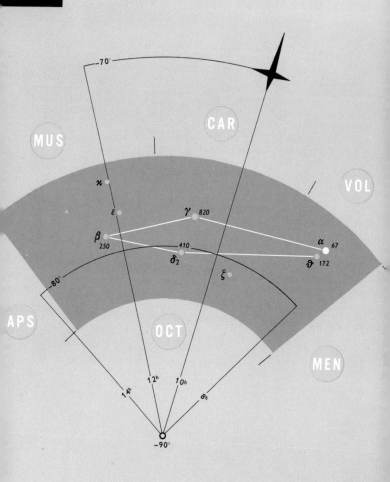

●5 ●4

MUS

CAR

VOL

APS

OCT

MEN

x

ε

γ 820

β
250

δ₂ 410

α 67

ϑ 172

ξ

−70°

−80°

−90°

14ʰ

12ʰ

10ʰ

8ʰ

CHAMAELEON

CIRCINUS

Circini   Cir   The Pair of Compasses

Perhaps from lack of imagination and in his incomprehensible desire to fill the southern sky with a great number of constellations at all costs, Abbé de La Caille designated one spot as the Pair of Compasses. This constellation has only one brighter star, the others having a magnitude of less than the 4th order. They could just as easily have been included in Centaurus or in Triangulum Australe, which are close to Circinus.

α **Circini,** at a distance of 57 light years, appears to a terrestrial observer as a star of magnitude 3.41. In the spectrum of this star the hydrogen lines are fainter and the metallic lines more intense. This is characteristic of the spectral type F0.

β **Circini.** All that is known of this star is that it has an apparent magnitude, or brightness, of 4.16. Other data are lacking.

γ **Circini,** at a distance of 270 light years, appears to a terrestrial observer as a star of magnitude 4.54. It has a composite spectrum B5 and F8 and absolute magnitude of −0.1, which is the same as the apparent brightness of Aldebaran in Taurus.

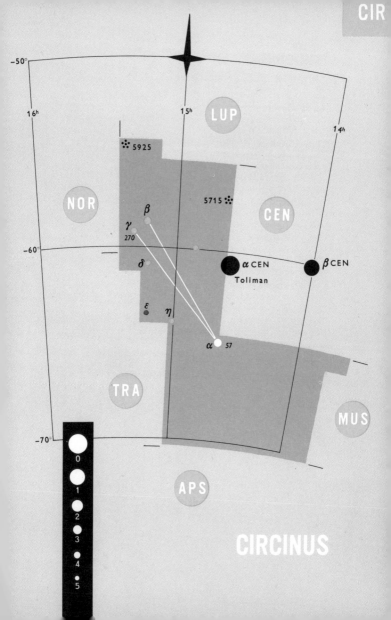

−50°

16ʰ

15ʰ

LUP

14ʰ

⚫ 5925

5715 ⚫

NOR

CEN

β

γ
270

−60°

δ

α CEN
Toliman

β CEN

ε   η

α   57

TRA

MUS

−70°

APS

CIRCINUS

0
1
2
3
4
5

COLUMBA
Columbae   Col   The Dove

This shapeless constellation was named by Royer in 1679 when he lived in the southern hemisphere. He saw it as a dove with a sprig in its bill.

α **Columbae,** or **Phakt** (the meaning is unknown), is the primary star of this constellation. It is 148 light years distant and has an apparent visual magnitude of 2.75. In fact it is a double star. The spectrum of the primary is B8. The second component is a faint star of approximately 12th magnitude.

β **Columbae** has an apparent magnitude of 3.22 but is really a sub-giant. The star lies at a distance of 120 light years and belongs to spectral group K1.

γ **Columbae** is 650 light years distant whence it appears to a terrestrial observer as a faint star of magnitude 4.36. If it were 10 parsecs (32.6 light years) distant it would shine like Venus at its brightest.

ε **Columbae** is a star of apparent visual magnitude of 3.92 lying at a distance of 250 light years. It belongs to spectral group K0.

Columba contains several extragalactic nebulae, objects that are of interest for photography rather than for visual observation.

It also contains a dark, light-absorbing cloud, through which, according to an unsubstantiated theory, the solar system passed at one time and which may have been the cause of the Ice Age on Earth.

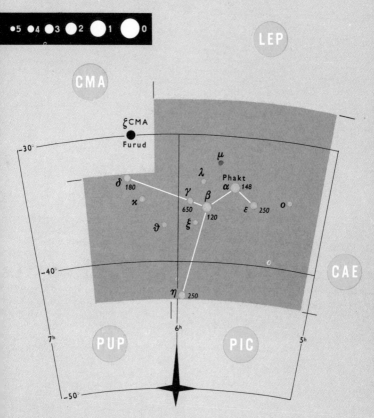

α CMA
Sirius

●5 ●4 ●3 ●2 ● 1 ● 0

LEP

CMA

ξCMA
Furud

-30°

μ
λ
δ 180
κ
γ 650
ϑ
ξ
β 120
Phakt
α 148
ε 250
o
η 250

-40°

CAE

7h
6h
5h

PUP
PIC

-50°

COLUMBA

COMA BERENICES
Comae Berenicis   Com   Berenice's Hair

The legend about Berenice, daughter of King Magas of Cyrene is a very old one. It was revived in the realm of astronomy by Tycho Brahe in his *Astronomiae Instauratae Progymnasmata* and has been retained to this day. Berenice, so the tale goes, had her beautiful locks shorn as a sacrifice to Venus in gratitude that her husband Ptolemy returned home safe and sound from the wars. Ptolemy was by no means overjoyed by this act on her part and only after the court mathematician Conon of Samos proclaimed that the gods had put the locks amongst the stars did they become reconciled. Neither ancient legend nor Tycho Brahe could have known that they thus delineated a part of the sky which contains a large cluster of distant galaxies. Coma Berenices is a constellation poor in stars.

α **Comae Berenicis,** called **Diadem,** is a star of magnitude 5.22, a dwarf of the spectral type F0. The temperature of such stars is somewhat higher than that of the Sun. The absolute brightness is 4.0, the distance 57 light years.

β **Comae Berenicis** is a dwarf star type G0, the spectrum being similar to that of the Sun. The apparent magnitude of this star, 27 light years distant from the Earth, is 4.32; the absolute magnitude is only 4.8.

γ **Comae Berenicis,** lying at a distance of 300 light years, appears to a terrestrial observer as a star of magnitude 4.56. It is an orange sub-giant of spectral class K3, which if it were 10 parsecs away would be as bright as a star of magnitude −0.2.

M 53 (NGC 5024) is a globular star cluster. The integrated brightness is 7.3 and it can be observed with good prismatic binoculars. Resolution of the individual stars in the cluster requires a telescope with at least 200-fold magnification, best of all a reflector telescope.

M 64 (NGC 4826) is a beautiful spiral nebula, bright as a star of magnitude 8.8.

M 85 (NGC 4382) is a spiral galaxy of 9th magnitude.

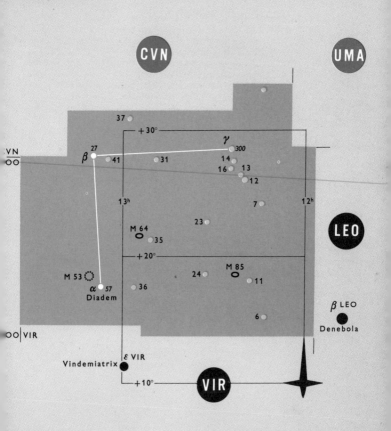

●5 ●4 ●3 ●2

CVN   UMA

37

+30°   γ
                              300
VN
OO   β 27   41   31   14
                                   16   13
                                        12
13h   12h

                                            7

            M 64   23
                35
                      +20°   LEO

M 53   24   M 85
            36   11   β LEO
α 57   Denebola
Diadem
                                              6
OO VIR

            ε VIR
Vindemiatrix

            +10°   VIR

COMA BERENICES

CORONA AUSTRALIS
Coronae Australis   CrA   The Southern Crown

The name Southern Crown was given, as a counterpart to the Northern Crown, to a group of stars forming a semicircle located below Sagittarius. It is quite prominent in the southern sky as it lies on the fringe of the Milky Way behind the sting of Scorpius. It lies in a region where the faintly luminous clouds of the Milky Way are interlaced with light-absorbing interstellar matter, consisting primarily of interstellar particles and interstellar gas. The scattering of radiation by the interstellar particles and its absorption by the gas reduces the stars' luminosity.

α **Coronae Australis** is a hydrogen star, spectral group A2, with apparent magnitude of 4.12, lying at a distance of 102 light years.

β **Coronae Australis** is a yellow-coloured star of spectral class G5, 365 light years distant. The apparent magnitude is 4.16, the absolute magnitude −1.1.

γ **Coronae Australis** is a dwarf star of spectral group F7 lying at a distance of 58 light years from the Earth whence it appears to an observer as a star of magnitude 4.26. At 10 parsecs it would be only one magnitude brighter.

δ **Coronae Australis** is an orange star, thus having its maximum intensity in the region of spectral line K1. It is 220 light years distant, and so appears to a terrestrial observer as a star of magnitude 4.66. The absolute magnitude is 0.5.

The constellation CrA also contains the globular star cluster **NGC 6541** — apparent brightness 5.8, apparent diameter 6 minutes of arc.

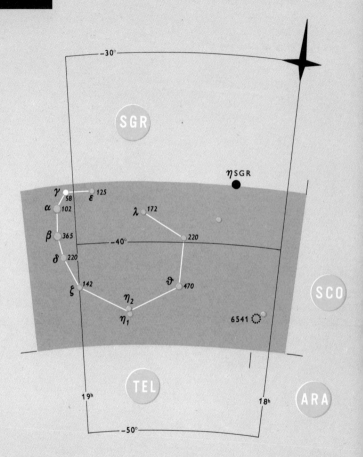

•5 ●4 ●3

−30°

SGR

η SGR

γ
ε 125
58
α
102
β
365
δ 220
ξ 142
λ 172
220
−40°
ϑ 470
η₂
η₁
6541

19ʰ

SCO

18ʰ

ARA

TEL

−50°

CORONA AUSTRALIS

CORONA BOREALIS
Coronae Borealis   CrB   The Northern Crown

This is a small but characteristic constellation comprising seven stars arranged in a semicircle resembling a diadem. The origin of the name dates from the distant past and is the subject of various legends, the most appealing perhaps being the one that Bacchus, wishing to convince Ariadne that he was a god, cast her headband into the sky.

α **Coronae Borealis,** or **Gemma,** Latin for 'precious stone', is the brightest star of the constellation with an apparent magnitude of 2.31 and absolute magnitude of 0.6. The A0 spectrum of this primary reveals that Gemma has a companion which revolves around it once in 17.4 days. α CrB is 71 light years distant.

β **Coronae Borealis** is a giant with an A8 spectrum lying at a distance of 102 light years. The apparent brightness is 3.72, the absolute brightness 1.2.

γ **Coronae Borealis** is a blue star, spectral type A0, 142 light years distant. The apparent brightness is 3.93, the absolute brightness 0.7.

ε **Coronae Borealis** is a giant star, spectral type K2, 172 light years away.

ϑ **Coronae Borealis** is a star of apparent magnitude 4.17, absolute magnitude 0.0, lying at a distance of 220 light years.

τ **Coronae Borealis** is a variable star, or rather a recurrent nova, which has exploded twice in 80 years. Its brightness increased to magnitude 2.0, thereupon diminishing to magnitude 15. The spectrum is Q-g M3, which indicates that this is a giant star of complex physical structure.

Corona Borealis also contains several faint double stars and variable stars.

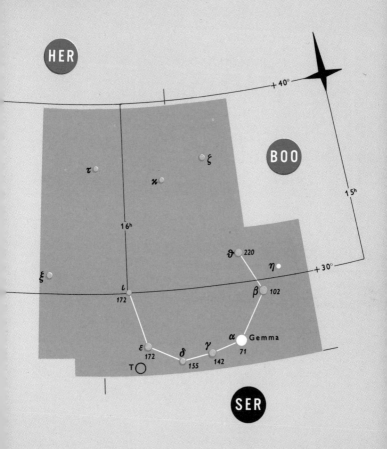

5 4 3 2

HER

BOO

ξ

τ

x

16ʰ

15ʰ

ξ

ϑ 220

η

+ 30°

β 102

ι
172

α Gemma
71

ε
172

δ
155

γ
142

T

SER

CORONA BOREALIS

+ 40°

CORVUS
Corvi   Crv   The Crow

Corvus is a small but prominent constellation consisting of seven stars forming a trapezium which appears to stand at an angle on the body of Hydra, the Sea Serpent. According to a legend Apollo sent the crow to bring the water of life. The crow, unable to resist the unripe fruits of the fig tree, let the cup fall to the ground and set to feasting. Realizing that he had loitered too long he snatched up the cup with his beak, a water snake with his claws, and hurried back to Apollo, offering a number of excuses for the delay. Apollo, however, knowing the truth, banished the whole group to the sky.

α **Corvi,** or **Alchita** (Al Chiba), meaning uncertain, is a dwarf star, spectral type F2, of apparent visual magnitude 4.18, lying at a distance of 63 light years. The absolute brightness is 2.8.

β **Corvi,** or **Kraz,** meaning uncertain, but probably referring to some part of the crow's body, is a giant star of the spectral class G4. At a distance of 172 light years its apparent magnitude is 2.84; the absolute magnitude is −0.8.

CRATER
Crateris   Crt   The Cup

Above the back of Hydra (The Water Snake) is the constellation known as The Cup. It is easily located below the star Denebola in Leo. Crater comprises six not very bright stars whose arrangement resembles the shape of a cup.

α **Crateris,** or **Alkes,** from the Arabic *al kas* meaning 'shallow basin', is a giant star of the spectral group K1 with an apparent visual magnitude of 4.20 and absolute magnitude of 0.7. It is 163 light years distant from the Earth.

β **Crateris,** is a type A2 star with apparent magnitude of 4.52, absolute magnitude 2.9. It takes 68 years for its light to reach the Earth.

γ **Crateris.** Its distance is 148 light years, spectrum A5, apparent brightness 4.14, absolute brightness 0.8.

Crater contains no details that can be observed with the unaided eye.

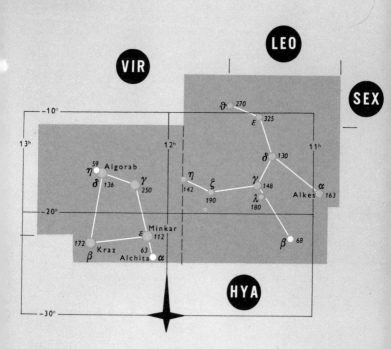

●5 ●4 ●3

LEO

VIR

SEX

−10°

13ʰ   12ʰ   11ʰ

η⁵⁹ Algorab
δ ¹³⁶   γ ²⁵⁰

η ¹⁴²   ξ ¹⁹⁰   γ ¹⁴⁸   α Alkes ¹⁶³
             δ ¹³⁰
        ϑ ²⁷⁰
          ε ³²⁵
             λ ¹⁸⁰

−20°

ε Minkar ¹¹²
β ¹⁷² Kraz   α ⁶³ Alchita   β ⁶⁸

HYA

−30°

CORVUS   CRATER

CRUX

Crucis   Cru   The Cross

Royer the sailor, and according to other sources Abbé de La Caille, devised the Southern Cross simply by selecting the four brightest stars in the constellation called Centaurus by the ancients. Bayer incorporated this name in his *Uranometria*, thus making it an officially recognized term.

Today the Southern Cross is one of the attractions for those who journey south. The brightness of its stars makes it a conspicuous constellation, and against the background of the Milky Way with its wealth of stars it is a true ornament of tropic nights.

α **Crucis,** or **Acrux,** is a double star. One component (α_1) has an apparent brightness of 1.58, the other (α_2) an apparent visual magnitude of 2.09. Both have a B1 spectrum and are 300 light years distant from the Earth. The first has an absolute magnitude of -3.4, the second -2.9.

β **Crucis** is another bright star in this constellation. It has an apparent brightness of 1.50, and the spectrum is also type B1; however the distance is 490 light years. The absolute magnitude is -4.5.

γ **Crucis** appears to a terrestrial observer as a star of magnitude 1.61. It is 220 light years distant and the absolute magnitude is -2.4. The spectrum is the characteristic one for red stars. The Harvard classification for it is M4.

δ **Crucis** is a fainter star of stellar magnitude 3.08 lying at a distance of 590 light years. The spectrum is that of helium stars with an effective temperature of 20,000°K. The absolute magnitude is -3.2.

ε **Crucis** is the fourth star of the Cross. Its spectrum is type K2, typical of orange stars, and it is 172 light years away. The apparent magnitude is 3.57, the absolute magnitude 0.0.

The Southern Cross contains many more, much fainter stars as well as numerous other objects, the brightest of which is the star cluster **NGC 4755** close to β Crucis.

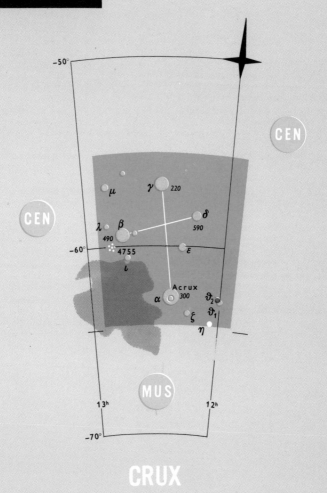

●5 ●4 ●3 ●2 ●1

CEN

CEN

μ

γ   220

δ
590

λ
β
490

ε

4755

ι

Acrux
α   300

ϑ₂

ϑ₁

ξ

η

13ʰ

12ʰ

−50°

−60°

−70°

MUS

CRUX

CYGNUS

Cygni   Cyg   The Swan

α **Cygni,** or **Deneb,** 'bird's tail', is the brightest star of the group. It is a super-giant of class A2 with an absolute brightness of −6.2, lying at a distance of 930 light years. If it were 10 parsecs distant, it would appear almost as bright as Canopus, the brightest star in the southern sky. The stellar magnitude of α Cygni is 1.33.

β **Cygni,** or **Albireo,** is a beautiful double star which can be observed with a small telescope. The two components are seen as two contrasting colours against the myriad of stars in the Milky Way. One is reddish-yellow because it is a giant star of the spectral type K1, the other is orange, of approximately the same spectral class. Both are 410 light years distant from the Earth.

γ **Cygni,** or **Sadir,** 'bird's breast', is a super-giant, spectral type F8. At a distance of 540 light years, the apparent magnitude is 2.32; the absolute magnitude is −3.5.

ε **Cygni,** or **Gienah,** 'wing', is a giant star, spectral type K0, with an apparent magnitude of 2.64 and absolute magnitude 0.7. Its distance is 80 light years.

χ **Cygni** is a long-period variable with apparent magnitude of 3.3, fading to 14th magnitude in a period of 407 days. It is a giant star, spectral type M7, lying at a distance of 230 light years.

P **Cygni,** on which Kepler wrote a monograph in 1606, is a nova-like variable waning to 6th magnitude from one of 3.3. It lies at a distance of 4700 light years.

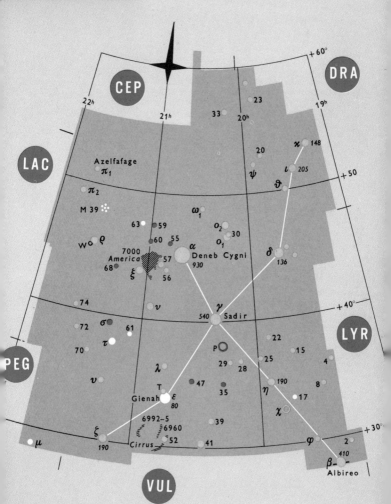

CYG

• 5 • 4 • 3 ● 2 ● 1

DRA

CEP

22h   21h   20h   19h

LAC

23

33   20

Azelfafage   π₁   κ 148

π₂   ψ   ι 205

+50°

M 39   ϑ

63 59   ω₁

Wo ρ   60 55   o₂   30

7000   57   α   o₁

America   68 ξ   56   Deneb Cygni   δ

930   136

74   ν   γ   Sadir

72 σ   61   +40°

22

70   τ   P   25   15

λ   29   28   4

υ   47   35   η 190   8

T   17

Gienah ε   χ

80

6992-5   6960   39

ξ   Cirrus   52   41   φ   2

μ   190   410

β
Albireo

PEG

LYR

VUL   CYGNUS

DELPHINUS

Delphini   Del   The Dolphin

Delphinus is a small attractive constellation comprising six stars. It lies east of the bright star Altair in Aquila on the fringe of the Milky Way with its myriads of stars.

The four stars α, β, γ and δ form a rhombus, the two other bright stars extending in a line to the west. There are several ancient legends associated with this constellation one of which tells that Delphinus is the son of the sea god Triton and that he saved the life of the singer Arion, whom he carried to dry land on his back.

α **Delphini,** called **Svalocin** (Sualocin), meaning unknown, is a blue dwarf of apparent magnitude 3.86, spectral type B8, lying at a distance of 270 light years. At a distance of 10 parsecs it would be as bright as Capella in Auriga.

β **Delphini,** called **Rotanev,** meaning unknown, is a dwarf star of spectral class F3, 96 light years distant, of absolute brightness 1.4.

γ_2 **Delphini** is a sub-giant of spectral class K1 with an apparent magnitude of 4.49 and absolute magnitude of 1.8. Light from this star takes 112 years to reach the Earth. The neighbouring star γ_1, 10.4 seconds away, is resolvable only with the aid of a telescope as a fainter component of magnitude 5.5. The absolute magnitude is 0.1.

δ **Delphini,** 250 light years away, is seen by a terrestrial observer as a star of magnitude 4.53.

ε **Delphini,** 270 light years distant, spectral class B7, has an apparent brightness of 3.98. At a distance of 10 parsecs it would be as bright as Capella in Auriga.

●5 ●4 ●3

VUL

SGE

PEG

γ 1,2
112
α Svalocin
270
δ
250
β 96
ξ
Rotanev
η 230
ε 270

x

+20°

+10°

EQU

AQL

21ʰ

20ʰ

AQR

AEQUATOR

0°

DELPHINUS

DORADO

Doradus   Dor   The Goldfish

This constellation is the easiest one to locate in the southern sky, as the Large Magellanic Cloud marks its southern borders. Dorado comprises four brighter stars.

α **Doradus** is a star of magnitude 3.47, spectral type A0 with surface temperature of about 10,000°K, lying at a distance of 300 light years.

β **Doradus** is a Cepheid variable with a period of 9.84 days, ranging between magnitudes 4.5 and 5.8. It is 910 light years distant.

γ **Doradus,** 47 light years distant, appears to a terrestrial observer as a star of magnitude 4.36. Physically it belongs to the group of stars with surface temperature greater than that of the Sun, i.e. of about 7500°K. The absolute magnitude is 3.6.

δ **Doradus** is a hydrogen star, spectral type A5. From a distance of 148 light years it shines as a star of magnitude 4.5. The absolute magnitude is 1.2.

LMC, the **Large Magellanic Cloud,** together with the **Small Magellanic Cloud** in Tucana were observed in 1519 by Magellan. They are sometimes called **Nubecula Major** and **Nubecula Minor.** Both clouds can be resolved into individual stars showing greater concentrations towards the centres. The brightest stars are of the 9th magnitude, the faintest of the 19th magnitude. Both clouds, which appear to belong to the Milky Way, contain several thousand variable stars, chiefly cepheids, a great number of star clusters, and large clouds of interstellar dust and gas. The Large Magellanic Cloud is most conspicuous in the gaseous nebula Tarantula and in other marginal parts of the cloud. The estimated distance is 64,000 parsecs. It seems that it participates in the rotation of the spiral arms of the Milky Way.

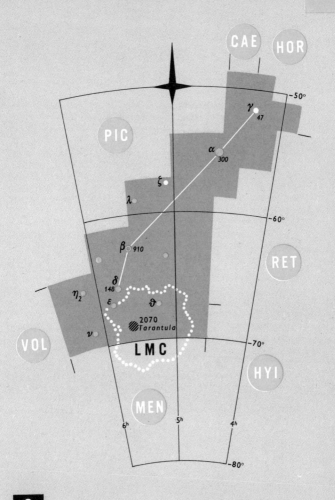

DOR

CAE   HOR

PIC

γ
47

α
300

ξ

λ

RET

β 910

η₂

δ
148

ε   ϑ

VOL

ν

2070
Tarantula

LMC

HYI

MEN

6ʰ   5ʰ   4ʰ

~50°

~60°

~70°

~80°

3
4
5

DORADO

DRACO
Draconis   Dra   The Dragon

According to mythology Draco is a reminder of the dragon Ladon in the garden of the Hesperides.

α **Draconis,** or **Thuban,** is a star of spectral class A. The spectrum indicates the presence of a companion which revolves around it once in 51 years. Thuban lies at a distance of 220 light years.

β **Draconis,** or **Alwaid,** is a star with physical properties resembling those of the Sun. It belongs to spectral class G2. At a distance of 10 parsecs it would appear brighter than Sirius to the terrestrial observer. β Draconis has a companion of the 14th magnitude. To a certain extent this double star is reminiscent of the relation between the Sun and Jupiter. It lies at a distance of 365 light years from the Earth.

γ **Draconis,** or **Etamin,** meaning 'dragon's head', is a red giant of spectral group K5 lying at a distance of 116 light years. It is the brightest star in the constellation with the luminosity of a star of magnitude 2.42. At a distance of 10 parsecs it would be brighter than Aldebaran.

δ **Draconis,** or **Nodus II,** is a yellow giant of class G8 lying at a distance of 120 light years. The apparent brightness is 3.24, the absolute magnitude 0.4.

ζ **Draconis,** or **Nodus I,** is a stellar giant of spectral group K3 seen by the terrestrial observer as a star of magnitude 3.90. It is 148 light years away and has an absolute magnitude of 1.4.

$v_{1,2}$ **Draconis,** or **Kuma,** is a double star with components of equal magnitude 5.0, belonging to the same spectral group; one is type A8 and the other A4. The two have a separation of 62 seconds and are 120 light years distant from the Earth.

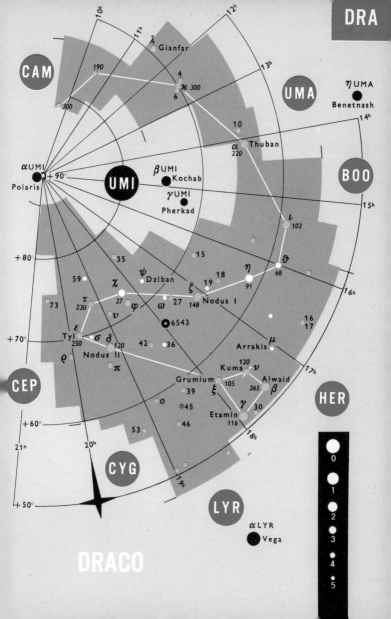

EQUULEUS

Equulei   Equ   The Foal

A superfluous constellation unknown either to Aratos or Cicero. It is of no interest except for four faint stars forming a trapezium south-east of Delphinus. One may try to resolve it on a fine summer night.

α **Equulei** is a spectroscopic binary with composite spectrum of class F6-A3. At a distance of 148 light years it shines like a star of magnitude 4.14. The primary star is a dwarf with an absolute magnitude of 0.8.

β **Equulei** is a star of barely 5.14 magnitude lying at a distance of 172 light years. The absolute magnitude is 1.5.

γ **Equulei** is a sub-giant of spectral group F1. To the terrestrial observer it seems as bright as a star of magnitude 4.76. At a distance of 10 parsecs it would be as bright as Aldebaran in Taurus. In reality, however, it lies at a distance of 180 light years from the Earth.

δ **Equulei** is a dwarf star, spectral type F3, apparent magnitude 4.61, 52 light years away. The absolute magnitude is 3.6.

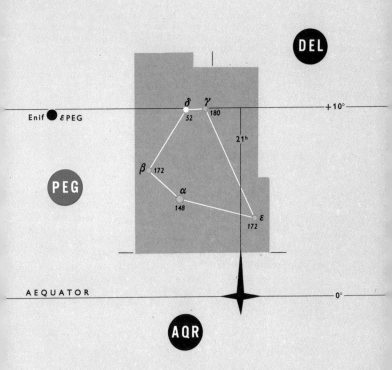

●5 ●4 ●3 ⬤2

DEL

δ γ
52 180

Enif ● εPEG   +10°

21ʰ

β ● 172

PEG

α
148

ε
172

AEQUATOR   0°

AQR

EQUULEUS

ERIDANUS

Eridani   Eri   The River Eridanus

According to Aratos, Eridanus is the river created by Phaeton, son of the Sun God. The Arabs also viewed it as a river, this being borne out by the name they gave it — Al Nahr. The names no longer used of the individual stars in Eridanus were of Arabic origin signifying, for example, a young ostrich, a nest on the bank of the river, etc.

Eridanus stretches west of Orion. It is a constellation of the southern sky but can be observed quite well to a considerable extent in the northern hemisphere as well.

α **Eri,** or **Achernar,** from the Arabic for 'river's end', has an apparent visual brightness of 0.6 and absolute brightness of −1.3. It lies at a distance of 78 light years. The spectral group is B9, the surface temperature 15,000°K. Achernar is two hundred times as bright as the Sun.

β **Eri,** or **Cursa,** from the Arabic for 'throne', is a star of spectral type A3 with apparent visual magnitude of 2.92 at a distance of 82 light years.

γ **Eri,** or **Zaurak,** is a red giant, spectral type M0 with an apparent brightness of 3.19 and absolute brightness of −2.4. It is 375 light years distant.

δ **Eri,** or **Rana,** is a dwarf star of spectral class K0 which at its distance of 29 light years is seen by a terrestrial observer as a star of magnitude 3.72. The absolute magnitude is 4.0.

ε **Eri** is also a dwarf, 11 light years away.

The other stars in Eridanus are generally faint ones. Popular science books frequently show a photograph of the typical **NGC 1300** nebula containing a barred spiral galaxy.

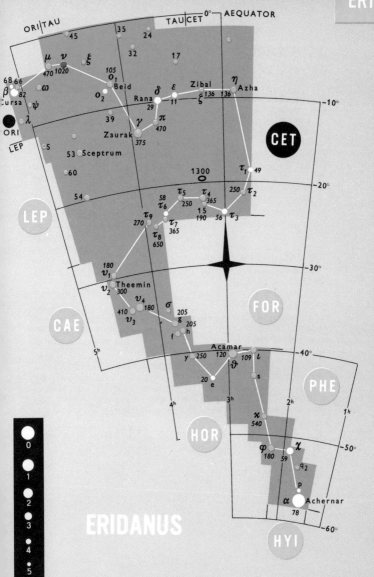

ERI

ORI|TAU   TAU|CET   0°   AEQUATOR

45   35   24

μ   ν   ξ
470 1020
68 66   ω   105   17
β   82   o₁   Beid   η
Cursa   ψ   o₂   Zibal   Azha
λ   Rana δ ε   ζ 136 136
ORI   29 γ π   11
LEP   39   Zaurak 470
S   375
53 Sceptrum

60   τ₁ 49

54   1300
                             O   250 τ₂
                      τ₅   τ₄   τ₃
                   58 τ₆ 250 365   15
                            τ₇ 190   56
                       τ₈ 365
                       650

LEP

                180
             υ₁
             υ₂ Theemin
                 300
                    υ₄ σ
             υ₃ 410 180   205
                            g 205
                            h
                         f
                    γ Acamar
                      250 120 ϑ 109 ι
                         20 e   s

FOR

CAE

HOR   κ
                    540

PHE

                    φ   χ
                180 59
                        q₂
                      p
                  α Achernar
                  78

ERIDANUS   HYI

CET

LEP

CAE

FOR

PHE

HOR

HYI

-10°

-20°

-30°

-40°

-50°

-60°

5ʰ   4ʰ   3ʰ   2ʰ   1ʰ

0
1
2
3
4
5

FORNAX

Fornacis   For   The Furnace

This constellation was introduced by the Abbé de La Caille; the original name Fornax Chemica was shortened to Fornax. It indicates the importance attributed to chemistry by his contemporaries of the 18th and 19th centuries. In Bode's atlas it is depicted realistically as a 'chemical furnace', though it requires a certain measure of imagination to see this shape in the few faint stars contained in this constellation. Fornax lies in a region of the sky rather lacking in stars in the direction of the southern horizon from the variable star Mira Ceti in Cetus (The Whale).

α **Fornacis** is a dwarf star, spectral type F5. Dwarfs are not miniature stars; the term is used to denote that they are of approximately the same size as the Sun. α Fornacis is 45 light years distant from our solar system. It shines as a star of magnitude 3.95.

β **Fornacis** is a yellow star, spectral type G6, lying at a distance of 148 light years. To a terrestrial observer it appears as bright as a star of magnitude 4.5. The absolute magnitude is 1.2.

ν **Fornacis,** 470 light years away, is a sub-giant of spectral type A0. It is as bright as a star of magnitude 4.74. At a distance of 10 parsecs it would have the brightness of a star of magnitude -1.0.

Passing through Fornax is a large, local system of galaxies which cannot be observed with the naked eye, but only by means of photography. It contains galaxies comprising millions of stars, centres of emission of gaseous matter and dust clouds which reflect the light of the stars.

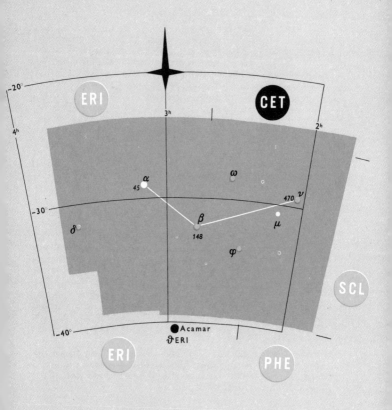

FOR

•5 •4 ●3

ERI

CET

ERI

SCL

PHE

-20°

4h

3h

2h

-30°

-40°

α
45

ω

ν
470

β
148

μ

δ

φ

Acamar
ϑ ERI

FORNAX

GEMINI
Geminorum   Gem   The Twins

Gemini is the third sign of the zodiac. It is a large constellation in which the ecliptic culminates. Planets can be best observed at this culminating point. Gemini lies between Cancer and Taurus. It is impossible to miss its two bright stars Castor and Pollux, the two brothers of mythology, originally called Dioscuri after their father Dios of Olympus.

α **Geminorum,** or **Castor,** is a complex system of stars. It shines as a star of magnitude 1.58 and a small telescope will resolve its companion of magnitude 2.89. Both have the bluish light characteristic of their respective spectra A2 and A0. A larger telescope will reveal a further star of 9th magnitude. All revolve around a common centre once in 380 years. Spectroscopic investigation has shown that each of the above stars has a further invisible companion so that in reality this is a sextuple system lying at a distance of 45 light years.

β **Geminorum,** or **Pollux,** is a giant star, spectral type K0, with a surface temperature of 4500°K. It is 35 light years distant from the Earth, and it shines as a star of magnitude 1.21. The absolute magnitude is 1.0.

γ **Geminorum,** or **Alhena,** called the Guard of the Pleiades, is a star of spectral class A1 lying at a distance of 84 light years. The visual magnitude is 1.93, the absolute magnitude -0.1.

ε **Geminorum,** or **Mebsuta,** 'outstretched arm', is a star of magnitude 3.18, which at a distance of 10 parsecs would be several times brighter than Sirius. However, as it is 1100 light years distant it is much fainter. In fact it is a super-giant of spectral class G8.

M 35 is a beautiful open star cluster which can be observed with opera glasses. When viewed through a larger telescope, the entire visual field is populated with stars of 8th to 12th magnitude.

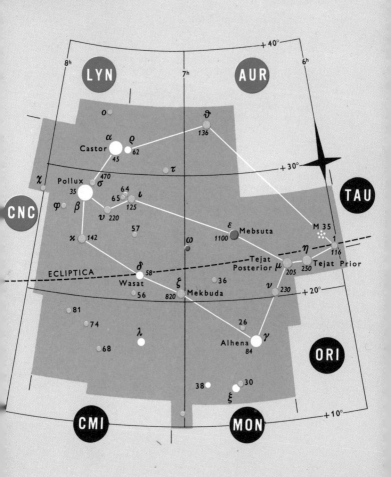

●5 ●4 ●3 ●2 ●1

LYN

AUR

TAU

CNC

ORI

CMI

MON

o

ϑ
136

α
Castor
45

ϱ
62

τ

+30°

χ

Pollux
35
470
σ

64

65
ι
125

φ

β

υ
220

57

ε
1100   Mebsuta

ω

M 35
1

η
116

κ
142

Tejat
Posterior μ
205

ν
250   Tejat Prior

ECLIPTICA

δ 58
Wasat
56

ξ
820   Mekbuda

36

ν
230

+20°

81

74

λ

26

68

Alhena
84
γ

38

30

ξ

+10°

8h

7h

6h

+40°

GEMINI

GRUS

Gruis   Gru   The Crane

This constellation lies south of the star Fomalhaut in Piscis Australis. It is not known who gave it the name Grus, for it was called Phoenicopterus, meaning 'flamingo', by older authors.

α **Gruis, Al Nair** or **Alnair,** Arabic for 'bright one'. This star is white, belonging to the spectral group B5. Al Nair is 91 light years distant from the Earth and glows in the southern sky with a brightness of magnitude 2.16. At a distance of 10 parsecs it would be as bright as a star of magnitude 0.3.

β **Gruis** is a lovely red colour characteristic of spectral group M6. The surface temperature, about 3500°K, is much lower than that of the Sun. At a distance of 270 light years it appears to a terrestrial observer as a star of magnitude 2.24. The absolute magnitude is -2.4.

γ **Gruis** lies at a distance of 163 light years and appears as a star of magnitude 3.6. However at one-fifth of this distance (10 parsecs), it would be as bright as a star of magnitude -0.3. It is a helium star of spectral class B8.

$\delta_1 \delta_2$ **Gruis** is an optical double, which means that the two components are only apparently close to each other. The first is a yellow star of the same spectral type as the Sun, the second a red star of spectral group M4. δ_1 is 230 light years away; the distance of the other star from the Earth has not been determined.

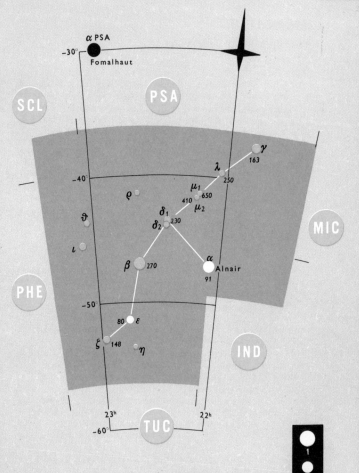

GRUS

HERCULES

Herculis   Her   Hercules

This constellation lies between Lyra and Corona Borealis (The Northern Crown). As the name implies it represents the legendary hero of Greek mythology.

α **Herculis,** or **Ras Algethi,** from the Arabic for 'kneeling man's head'. Ras Algethi is a red giant of spectral class M5. It is a double star and was resolved with a telescope as early as 1779 by Maskelyne. The primary is 800 times as large as the Sun and the second component, also a giant, is an intense blue. Data as to the colour of binaries are not always reliable. Changes in the spectrum of the primary indicate the existence of a third component which revolves around the star once in 52 years. The whole system is about 540 light years distant.

β **Herculis, Antilicus** or **Rutilicus** (the meaning is uncertain; according to Bayer's atlas it is 'lion skin'). This is a giant star of spectral class G8, apparent magnitude 2.81, absolute magnitude −0.2, lying at a distance of 125 light years.

γ **Herculis** is a dwarf star, type A6, 142 light years distant from the Earth. The apparent visual magnitude is 3.79, the absolute magnitude 0.6.

δ **Herculis,** or **Sarin,** (in Bayer's *Uranometria* the star Sarin denotes the shoulder). This is a blue star, spectral type A3, apparent brightness 3.16, absolute brightness 0.6, lying at a distance of 105 light years.

g **Herculis** is a semi-regular variable ranging between magnitudes 4.6 and 6.0 with a period of about 70 days. It is a giant star of spectral group M2, 410 light years away.

M 13 is the loveliest globular star cluster in the northern sky. It can just be made out with the naked eye between η and ζ Herculis. A small or medium-size telescope makes it a sight to behold. Greater magnification resolves the cluster into a myriad of stars. The estimated distance is 3000 light years.

M 92 is another globular star cluster in Hercules, which is 3300 light years distant.

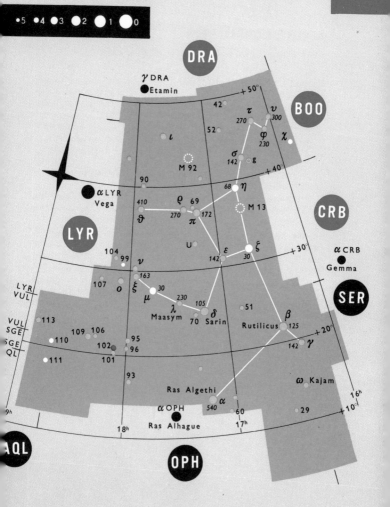

• 5 • 4 ● 3 ● 2 ● 1 ● 0

DRA

BOO

γ DRA
● Etamin

42

τ

υ
300

52

φ
230

χ

ι

σ
142

g

M 92

+ 50°

+ 40°

68

η

90

ρ

69

M 13

α LYR
Vega

410

270

η

CRB

LYR

ϑ

π
172

α CRB
Gemma

U

ε
142

ξ
30

+ 30°

104

99

ν

SER

107

o

ξ

163

30

μ

230

λ

105

51

β

Maasym

70 Sarin

δ

Rutilicus

125

+ 20°

VUL
SGE

113

109

106

95

142

γ

SGE
QL

110

102

96

ω Kajam

111

101

93

Ras Algethi

29

9h

18h

α OPH
Ras Alhague

540

α

60

17h

16h

+ 10°

AQL

OPH

HERCULES

HOROLOGIUM
Horologii   Hor   The Pendulum Clock

In making his additions to the constellations of the southern sky, Abbé de La Caille introduced The Pendulum Clock between Eridanus, near Achernar, and the constellation Reticulum. It is a long, inconspicuous constellation, for it contains few stars, generally of the 4th and 5th magnitude.

α **Horologii** is the brightest star, having a magnitude of 3.83; it is 148 light years distant from the Sun. It has a K1 spectrum with intense metallic lines and molecular absorption bands. The surface temperature is 4500°K, the absolute magnitude 0.5.

β **Horologii** is a hydrogen star. Its distance from the Earth is not known exactly. To a terrestrial observer it has the luminosity of a star of almost 5th magnitude.

η **Horologii** is almost beyond the limits of the range of this atlas for it has a brightness of 5.26. It has a high temperature as is the case in stars of spectral class A5. The distance from the Earth is 155 light years.

μ **Horologii** is 155 light years away. It belongs to spectral class F0 where the hydrogen lines become fainter and the metallic lines more intense. The temperature, 7500°K, is higher than that of the Sun.

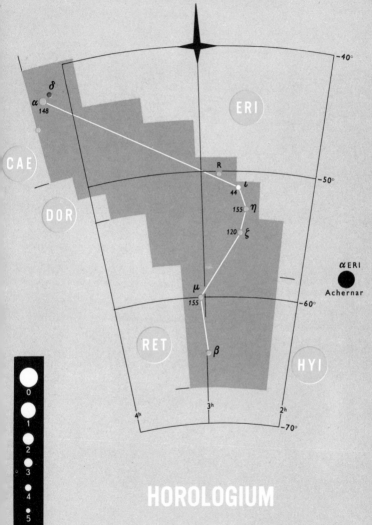

HOROLOGIUM

HYDRA

Hydrae   Hya   The Water Snake

The Water Snake is the longest constellation in both the southern and northern sky. The head, which rises above the celestial equator, begins below Cancer, drops below the equator and extends to Libra.

α **Hydrae,** or **Alfard,** is a giant of spectral classification K3, 130 light years distant. The absolute brightness is −1.0 but to the terrestrial observer it has the brightness of a star of magnitude 2.16.

β **Hydrae,** 270 light years away, shines as a star of magnitude 4.40. It belongs to spectral group B9 and has an absolute magnitude of −0.2.

γ **Hydrae** has an apparent brightness of 3.33, lies at a distance of 130 light years and is a giant of spectral type A0. The absolute magnitude is 0.3.

δ **Hydrae** is a blue star A0, 130 light years away, with an apparent magnitude of 4.18 and absolute magnitude 1.2.

ε **Hydrae** is a dwarf of spectral group G0 and is 136 light years distant from the Earth. The apparent brightness is 3.48, the absolute brightness 0.2.

ζ **Hydrae** is a yellow giant 130 light years away. At this distance it shines as a star of magnitude 3.30; at 10 parsecs it would be as bright as Vega.

η **Hydrae** belongs to spectral class B5 and shines as a star of magnitude 4.32 from its distance of 410 light years. If it were 10 parsecs distant, it would be as bright as a star of magnitude −1.2.

R Hydrae is the designation for a variable star with a long period of 387 days during which it ranges between stellar magnitudes 4.0 and 10.0.

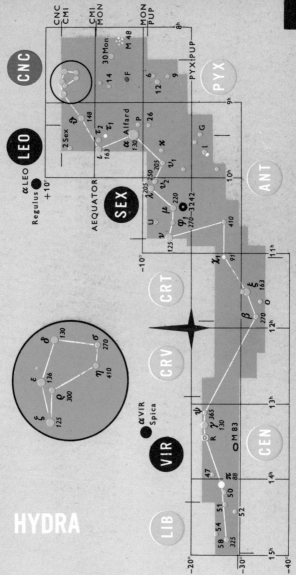

HYA

HYDRA

CNC
LEO
SEX
CRT
CRV
VIR
LIB

PYX
ANT
CEN

CNC
CMI
CMI
MON
MON
PUP
PYX|PUP

8ʰ

30 Mon
M 48
14
τ₁
F
6
12
9

9ʰ

148
ϑ
τ₂
26
P
2 Sex
ι
163
α Alfard
130
κ
ν₁
I
G

+10°
Regulus
α LEO

AEQUATOR
λ 205
ν₂ 150
205
v₂ 220
μ
U
φ₁ 270-3242
ν
125
410

-10°
χ₁
91
ξ
163
β
270
O

10ʰ

11ʰ

12ʰ

δ 130
σ 270
ε
136
η 410
ρ 300
ξ 125

α VIR
Spica

ψ 365
R γ 130
M 83
47
π 88
50
51
52
58 54 51
325

13ʰ

14ʰ

15ʰ

-20°
-30°
-40°

• 5 • 4 • 3 ● 2 ● 1

HYDRUS

Hydri   Hyi   The Lesser Water Snake

This constellation lies near the Large Magellanic Cloud. Johann Bayer introduced it in 1603 as the counterpart of the large constellation Hydra, visible also in the northern sky. Hydrus is an inconspicuous constellation, its brightest star being located above Achernar at the end of the river Eridanus.

α **Hydri** lies at a distance of 41 light years. Physically it belongs to spectral group A7, i.e. the hydrogen stars, whose surface temperature is very high, about 20,000°K. It shines in the heavens as a star of magnitude 3.02. The absolute magnitude is 2.5.

β **Hydri** is a dwarf star of the solar type G0 seen by a terrestrial observer at a distance of 22 light years as a star of magnitude 2.90. The absolute magnitude is 3.8.

γ **Hydri,** 250 light years away, has an apparent magnitude of 3.17, absolute magnitude −1.3. It is of spectral class M3, characterized by molecular bands, and has a lower temperature of about 3500°K.

δ **Hydri** is a hydrogen star of type A2, lying at a distance of 72 light years, and appears to a terrestrial observer as a star of magnitude 4.26. The absolute magnitude is 2.5.

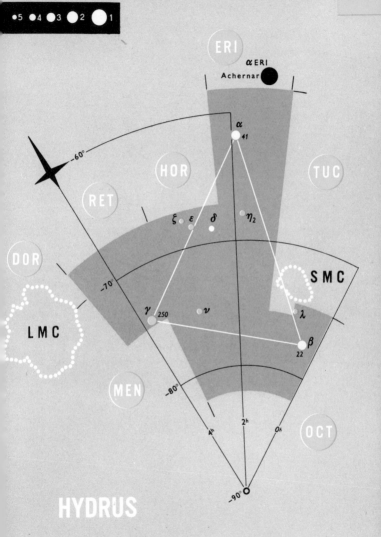

HYI

ERI

α ERI
Achernar

HOR

TUC

RET

ξ ε δ   η₂

DOR

SMC

LMC

γ 250   ν   λ

β 22

MEN

OCT

HYDRUS

INDUS

Indi   Ind   The Indian

This constellation was first depicted in Bayer's *Uranometria* in 1603. The Latin name Indus more correctly denotes an inhabitant of India, but the shape of the constellation resembles a North American Indian. It is an inconspicuous figure in the southern sky; four somewhat brighter stars may be observed between Pavo and Grus.

α **Indi** is a star of the same spectral class as our Sun, which means that it has about the same surface temperature, about 6000°K. If the star has a chromosphere, then it may be assumed that the same phenomena occur there as on the Sun. Eruptive prominences would occur and matter would fall back on to the star from the corona, which it may be assumed to possess. Lying at a distance of 102 light years α Indi appears to the terrestrial observer as a star of magnitude 3.21. The absolute magnitude is 0.7.

β **Indi** is a much cooler star with a temperature of about 4500°K, metallic lines being predominant in its spectrum K2. It is 270 light years distant. The star's brightness is 3.72, the absolute brightness is −0.9.

δ **Indi** is a yellowish star 190 light years away. It is a double with components of magnitude 4.60 (the primary) and 7.0. The total brightness of the two components is 4.60. They have a separation of 5.3 seconds; in other words they can be resolved only with a medium-large telescope.

ϑ **Indi** is a star of magnitude 4.60 lying at a distance of 78 light years. It is a hydrogen star, type A5, with an effective surface temperature of approximately 10,000°K.

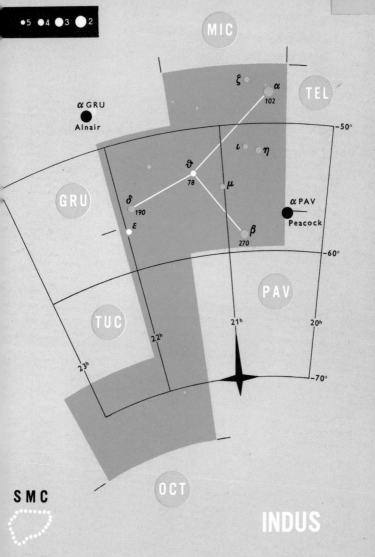

IND

●5 ●4 ●3 ●2

MIC

ξ

α
102

TEL

α GRU
Alnair

ι   η

−50°

GRU

ϑ
78

μ

δ
190

α PAV
Peacock

ε

β
270

−60°

PAV

TUC

22ʰ

21ʰ

20ʰ

23ʰ

−70°

SMC

OCT

INDUS

LACERTA

Lacertae   Lac   The Lizard

This is another constellation introduced to fill a gap in the sky. Hevelius gave the name Lacerta to a group of stars lying between Cygnus and Andromeda. The constellation contains few stars, is not conspicuous in any way and is therefore difficult to locate. The following are three of the brighter stars:

α **Lacertae** has a high effective temperature of about 10,000°K. It is a hydrogen star of spectral class A0, lying at a distance of 91 light years. The stellar magnitude is 3.85, the absolute magnitude 1.6.

β **Lacertae** is a stellar giant of spectral group K0, 172 light years distant. To a terrestrial observer it is as bright as a star of magnitude 4.58. The absolute visual magnitude is 1.0.

1 **Lacertae** is also a giant, spectral type K4, 325 light years away. Viewed from the Earth, it has an apparent magnitude of 4.22. The absolute magnitude is of a negative order, viz. −0.8. which means that the star is in reality far brighter.

Lacerta contains no bright objects. The only remarkable phenomenon was the recent appearance (1910) of novae, mostly of spectral class Q; the brightest, **CP Lacertae,** dates from 1950 when it attained a stellar magnitude of 2.1, and faded within a few months to magnitude 14.4.

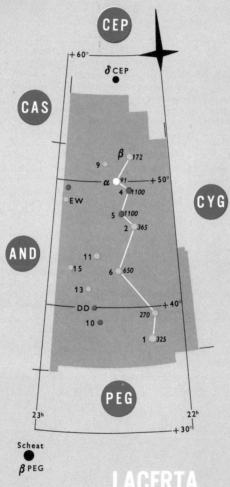

●5 ●4 ●3 ○2

CEP

δ CEP

CAS

β 172

9

α 91 +50°

4 1100

EW

5 1100

CYG

2 365

AND

11

15

6 650

13

DD +40°

270

10

1 325

PEG

23ʰ

22ʰ

+30°

Scheat
β PEG

LACERTA

LEO

Leonis   Leo   The Lion

On the descending part of the ecliptic lies the constellation Leo, fourth sign of the zodiac. Leo is associated with the legends of Hercules, namely the one in which he strangles the Nemean lion as one of his twelve labours.

α **Leonis,** or **Regulus.** According to Pliny this star was called Stella Regina, most probably because it lies directly on the ecliptic and because there are frequent conjunctions and appulses with planets or the Moon at this point. Regulus has an apparent visual magnitude of 1.34 and an absolute magnitude of −0.2. It is a helium star with an effective surface temperature of about 20,000°K. It is 68 light years distant.

β **Leonis,** or **Denebola,** the Arabic name meaning 'lion's tail'. This is the second brightest star in this constellation and lies 42 light years away. It is a hydrogen star, spectral type A4, with a surface temperature of about 20,000°K. The apparent magnitude is 2.23 and the absolute magnitude is 1.6.

γ **Leonis,** or **Algieba,** Arabic for 'lion's mane', is a system of two giant stars, one orange and the other yellow, revolving around a common centre of gravity once in a period of 619 years. The primary is of spectral type K0, the second component of spectral type G5. The system is 130 light years distant from the Earth. The primary star has an apparent magnitude of 2.61 and absolute magnitude of −0.4.

δ **Leonis,** or **Zosma.** The name is of uncertain origin, perhaps Persian, and may mean 'girdle'. It belongs to spectral class A2, shining from its distance of 68 light years with the luminosity of a star of magnitude 2.58. The absolute magnitude is 0.1.

Leo contains several bright nebulae: **M 65, M 66, M 95** and **M 96,** which lie outside our Galaxy.

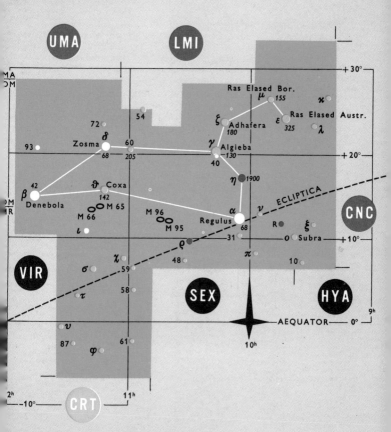

LEO

●5 ●4 ●3 ●2 ●1

UMA   LMI

Ras Elased Bor.
μ 155   ϰ
                              Ras Elased Austr.
72   54   ξ   ε 325
        δ   Adhafera 180   λ
93   Zosma 60   γ Algieba
        68   205   40 130   +20°
                                    η 1900
    β   42   ϑ Coxa
Denebola   142   ν ECLIPTICA
        ○ ○ M 65   α   CNC
    ι M 66   M 96 ○ ○   Regulus 68   R   ξ
                M 95   31   o   Subra +10°
VIR   ρ   π   10
        χ   59   48   HYA
    σ   58
    τ   SEX
                                        AEQUATOR 0°
    υ   9h
87   φ   61   10h

2h -10°
        CRT

LEO

LEO MINOR

Leonis Minoris   LMi   The Lesser Lion

Leo Minor is the designation of a few faint stars lying above the head of Leo. This constellation appeared for the first time in the *Prodromus Astronomiae* of Hevelius in 1690. It is best located by looking for it between Ursa Major and Leo. Leo Minor comprises the following stars:

β **Leonis Minoris** is a giant of spectral class G8 with an apparent visual magnitude of 4.41. The absolute magnitude is 0.6, and at a distance of 10 parsecs β LMi would be as bright as Capella in Auriga. However, as it is 190 light years distant, it appears to a terrestrial observer as a star of lower apparent magnitude.

21 Leonis Minoris is a giant of spectral group A5, apparent magnitude 4.47, absolute magnitude -1.6, lying at a distance of 120 light years.

10 Leonis Minoris is a yellow giant, spectral type G6, glowing in the sky at a distance of 172 light years as a star of magnitude 4.62.

o **Leonis Minoris** is a dwarf star of spectral class K2 with an apparent magnitude of 3.92 and absolute magnitude of 1.4, lying at a distance of 102 light years.

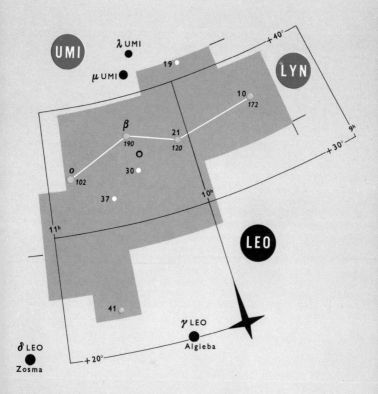

●5 ●4 ●3 ●2

UMI

λ UMI

μ UMI

19

LYN

10
172

β
190

21
120

9ʰ

+ 40°

+ 30°

o
102

30

10ʰ

37

11ʰ

+ 20°

LEO

41

γ LEO
Algieba

δ LEO
Zosma

LEO MINOR

LEPUS

Leporis   Lep   The Hare

This is a fairly prominent constellation which is easy to find because it lies below the stars Saiph and Rigel in Orion. The Hare symbolizes the speed with which the Greek god Hermes (Roman god Mercury) is credited. The chief stars in Lepus are as follows:

α **Leporis,** or **Arneb,** from the Arabic *al arnab* meaning 'hare', is a super-giant, spectral type F0, which observed from the Earth has a brightness of 2.69. It is 410 light years away; if it were 10 parsecs distant it would be brighter than Spica in Virgo.

β **Leporis,** or **Nihal,** is a yellow giant of spectral class G2, lying at a distance of 180 light years; it is seen by a terrestrial observer as a star of magnitude 2.96. At 10 parsecs it would be as bright as α Eridani or Achernar.

γ **Leporis,** at a distance of 27 light years, shines as a star of magnitude 3.80. It is a dwarf which would show little increase in brightness at 10 parsecs. It is also a double star with components of magnitudes 3.8 and 6.4.

ε **Leporis,** unlike the preceding star, is a giant of spectral type K5, but is equally bright from its distance of 220 light years. However, at 10 parsecs it would be as bright as Capella in Auriga.

Lepus contains several other double stars as well as variable stars and star clusters, but none is bright enough to be included in this guide. An exception is made however in the case of **M 79** (NGC 1904), as it is a magnificent spherical star cluster, unusually rich in stars. Viewed with a small telescope it looks like a hazy cloud; but a larger instrument will resolve it into a large number of sparkling stars.

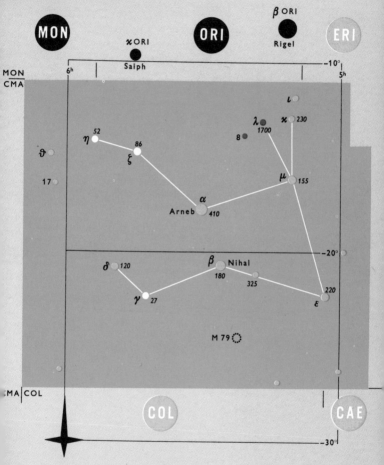

LEP

●5 ●4 ●3 ●2 ●1 ●0

MON   **x** ORI   ORI   β ORI
           Saiph   Rigel   ERI

MON
CMA   6ʰ   -10°   5ʰ

                                              ι
                                    λ   x ⟩ 230
                                   1700
                         8
η ⟩ 52
         86   μ ⟩ 155
ϑ   ξ

17   α
            Arneb ⟩ 410

                                                    -20°
δ ⟩ 120   β   Nihal
                  180   325
    γ ⟩ 27   220
                                                    ε

                M 79

CMA COL   CAE
           COL

                                            -30°

LEPUS

LIBRA

Librae   Lib   The Scales

Libra is the seventh sign of the zodiac. It contains several faint stars. At one time they were part of Scorpius and went by the name of Chelae, Scorpion's Claw. The Scales were included among the signs of the zodiac in honour of the Roman Consul Julius Caesar, for his reform of the Roman calendar and his reputed justice.

α **Librae,** or **Zuben Elgenubi** (Zubenelgenubi), the southern claw of Scorpius according to the Arabs, who did not know the new name for this section of the sky. The star has an apparent brightness of 2.90. The nearby star has a different spectrum; the primary belongs to group A3, the other to spectral class F4. The first is 62 light years distant, the second 78 light years.

β **Librae,** or **Zuben Elschemali** (Zubeneschamali), from the Arabic for 'the northern claw of Scorpius', lying at a distance of 148 light years, glows as a star of magnitude 2.74. The spectrum B8 is that of a helium star; it also indicates the existence of an unseen companion revolving around the primary in a period of 80 days.

γ **Librae,** or **Zuben Elakrab** (Zubenelakrab), is a giant star 109 light years away. The apparent magnitude is 4.02, the absolute magnitude is 4.1. The spectrum G6 is like that of our Sun.

δ **Librae** or **Zuben Elakribi** is a variable star ranging between magnitudes 4.8. and 5.9 in a period of 2.33 days. The star belongs to spectral group A0 and is 205 light years away.

Listed in the Messier catalogue under the number **M 5** and in the New General Catalogue under the number **NGC 5897** is a spherical star cluster which is visible with a small telescope.

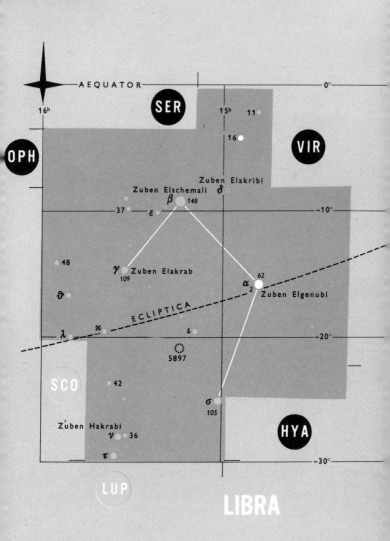

LIB

● 5 ● 4 ● 3 ● 2

AEQUATOR

SER

OPH

VIR

16h

15h   11

16

Zuben Elakribi

Zuben Elschemali   δ

β   148

37   ε

62

α   2

Zuben Elgenubi

48

γ   Zuben Elakrab

109

ϑ

ECLIPTICA

λ   κ   ι

−10°

−20°

5897

SCO

42

σ

105

Zuben Hakrabi

ν   36

HYA

τ

−30°

LUP

LIBRA

LUPUS
Lupi   Lup   The Wolf

According to legend this constellation is the animal into which the blood-thirsty King Lycaon of Arcadia was turned.

α **Lupi** is a star of magnitude 2.89, 820 light years distant from the Earth. The spectrum B2 indicates that it is a helium star with an effective surface temperature of about 20,000°K. At a distance of 10 parsecs (32.6 light years), it would be as bright as α Crucis.

β **Lupi** belongs to the same spectral class, namely B3. From its position 270 light years away it shines as a star of magnitude 2.81. The absolute magnitude is −1.8.

γ **Lupi** is of spectral type B3 with an apparent visual magnitude of 2.95. Light from this star takes about 230 years to reach the Earth. The absolute magnitude is −1.3.

δ **Lupi** is a helium star which shines in the sky as a star of magnitude 3.43. It is 270 light years distant; the absolute magnitude is −1.2.

ε **Lupi** is 540 light years distant and has an apparent brightness of 3.74. ε Lupi is of spectral class B3, a helium star, like most of the stars in this constellation, with a surface temperature of approximately 20,000°K. If it were 10 parsecs distant, it would be as bright as α Crucis.

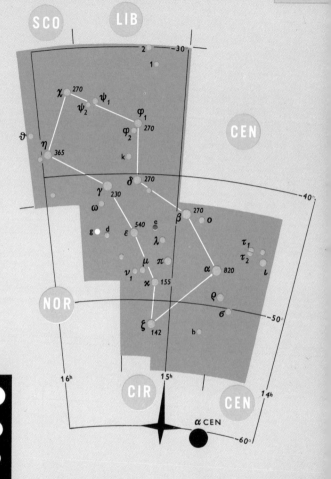

LUP

SCO   LIB

CEN

2 −30°
1

χ 270   ψ₁
ψ₂   φ₁
           φ₂ 270
ϑ
η 365   k
           δ 270
γ 230
ω   β 270   o
g d ε 540 e
        λ   τ₁
μ π   τ₂ ι
ν₁   α 820
κ 155   ϱ
NOR   σ
ξ 142   b   −50°
16ʰ   15ʰ   14ʰ
CIR   CEN
α CEN −60°

0
1
2
3
4
5

LUPUS

LYNX

Lyncis   Lyn   The Lynx

In 1690 Johannes Hevelius, Mayor of Danzig, introduced into this barren region a constellation to which he gave the name Lynx. It comprises a scattered group of faint stars lying between Gemini and Ursa Major.

α **Lyncis,** with a magnitude of 3.30, is the brightest star in the constellation. It is a red giant, of spectral type M0, lying at a distance of 172 light years. At 10 parsecs it would be as bright as Rigel in Orion.

31 Lyncis is a giant, of spectral type G0-A3 indicative of the spectroscopic component of a binary system. At its distance of 220 light years it has an apparent magnitude of 4.43. The absolute brightness is 0.3.

38 Lyncis is a helium star of spectral type B9, with an effective surface temperature of about 20,000°K. Lying at a distance of 109 light years, it shines as a star of magnitude 3.82. The absolute brightness is 1.2.

15 Lyncis, magnitude 4.54, is a giant of spectral type G6, 230 light years away. The absolute magnitude is the same as the apparent magnitude of Rigel in Orion.

21 Lyncis, at a distance of 250 light years, shines as a star of magnitude 4.45. It is a hydrogen star of spectral type A0; the temperature of these stars is usually about 10,000°K. The absolute magnitude is 0.0.

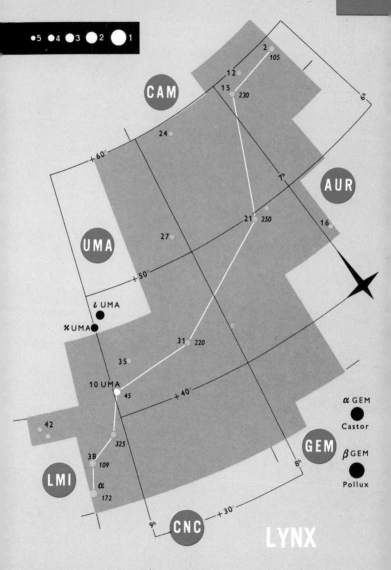

CAM

AUR

UMA

2
105

12

15
230

24

16

21
250

27

ι UMA

κ UMA

31
220

35

10 UMA
45

42

38
109

325

α
172

α GEM
Castor

β GEM
Pollux

GEM

LMI

CNC

LYNX

+ 60°

+ 50°

+ 40°

+ 30°

6ʰ

7ʰ

8ʰ

9ʰ

●5 ●4 ●3 ●2 ●1

LYRA
Lyrae   Lyr   The Lyre

This is a small but conspicuous constellation of the summer sky. The chief star is Vega. Lyra lies outside the main stream of the Milky Way but in a region still rich in stars. The original Greek name for this constellation was Chélys, meaning 'shell of a tortoise', from which Hermes made a stringed instrument which he gave to Orpheus. After the latter's death Zeus placed the lyre amongst the stars.

α **Lyrae,** or **Vega,** 'string instrument'. The Arabs called this star 'the falling eagle'. After Arcturus in Boötes, Vega is the brightest star in the northern sky. The spectrum A1 is typical of hydrogen stars with an effective surface temperature of about 10,000°K. The apparent magnitude is 0.14; the absolute magnitude is −0.5. It lies at a distance of 26 light years from the Earth.

$\beta_1\beta_2$ **Lyrae,** or **Sheliak.** This star is a typical variable, the two components being elongate in all probability. It is continuously changing in brightness and the period also has irregular fluctuations — currently it is 12 days 22 hours 23 minutes. Some observers presume the existence of pulsating gas shells in the case of both stars. The star ranges in brightness between magnitudes 3.4 and 4.3. The spectrum indicates that both are hydrogen stars. The distance from the Earth is 1100 light years.

$\varepsilon_1\ \varepsilon_{1,2}$ **Lyrae** are stars of spectral group A which form a triple system. All are 206 light years away.

M 57 or **NGC 6720** is the designation of the planetary nebula observed by Darquier in 1779. It is distinguished by a sharp ring outline which can be observed with a medium-large telescope. In the centre of the nebula is a very hot star whose short-wave radiation causes the ring to become luminous. Photographs made in a red light reveal filaments along the whole length of the nebula's major axis.

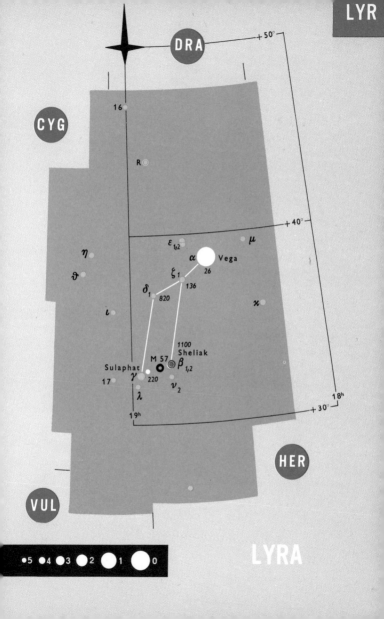

LYR

DRA

+50°

CYG

16

R

+40°

η

ϑ

ε₁,₂

μ

α Vega

ξ₁

26

136

δ₁

820

ι

x

1100
Sheliak

M 57

β₁,₂

Sulaphat

γ

220

ν₂

17

λ

19ʰ

+30°

18ʰ

HER

VUL

LYRA

•5 •4 ●3 ●2 ● 1 ● 0

MENSA

Mensae   Men   The Table Mountain

Abbé de La Caille immortalized his observatory on Table
Mountain by placing it among the constellations in his
Coelum Australe Stelliferum. Mensa is not rich in stars, but
de La Caille introduced it to fill in a region in the sky. It
contains the following stars:

α **Mensae** is a star on the threshold of naked eye visibility,
for it has an apparent magnitude of 5.14. The spectral
class is G6. It is a dwarf of the group to which our Sun also
belongs. Light from α Mensae takes 28 years to reach the
Earth.

β **Mensae** is a faint star of magnitude 5.30 covered by the
splendid gaseous nebula Tarantula which lies for the most
part within the borders of the constellation Dorado. Its
distance from the Earth is 136 light years.

γ **Mensae,** lying at a distance of 220 light years, shines as
a star of magnitude 5.06. The spectrum is K4, the absolute
magnitude 0.9.

η **Mensae** is the last of the stars in the Table Mountain.
190 light years away, it has an apparent magnitude of 5.28
and an absolute magnitude of 1.4.

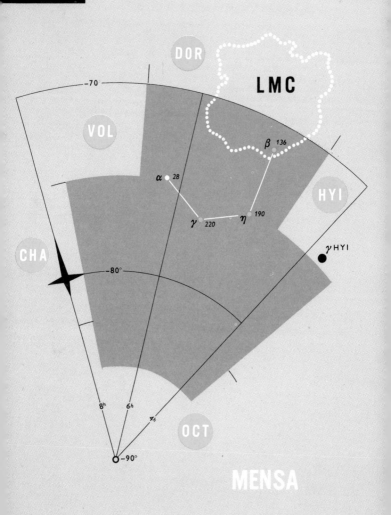

●5 ●4 ○3

MEN

DOR

LMC

VOL

β 136

α 28

HYI

γ 220   η 190

γ HYI

CHA

−70

−80°

8ʰ   6ʰ

4ʰ

OCT

−90°

MENSA

MICROSCOPIUM

Microscopii   Mic   The Microscope

This constellation introduced by de La Caille depicts the microscope, the instrument which revolutionized the study of medicine and natural science in the 18th century. Unfortunately this minor monument in the sky is not equal in importance to the instrument. The constellation comprises several stars of barely 5th magnitude which lie between Pavo and Volans.

α **Microscopii** is a solar type star with spectrum G6 and a somewhat lower temperature than that of the Sun. The apparent magnitude is 5.0; the distance from the Earth is 365 light years. If it were 10 parsecs distant, it would be as bright as Arcturus, the main star in Boötes.

γ **Microscopii,** with an absolute magnitude of 0.4, is the brightest star of this group even though the apparent magnitude is 4.71. The spectral class, like that of the preceding star, is G4. It is 230 light years away.

ε **Microscopii** is the last of the three stars which delineate this constellation. The apparent magnitude is 4.79, the absolute magnitude is 2.1, and the distance from the Earth is 112 light years. The spectrum is typical of hydrogen stars with a surface temperature of about 10,000°K. Stars of this type are white and comprise 27 per cent of the total number of stars in the heavens.

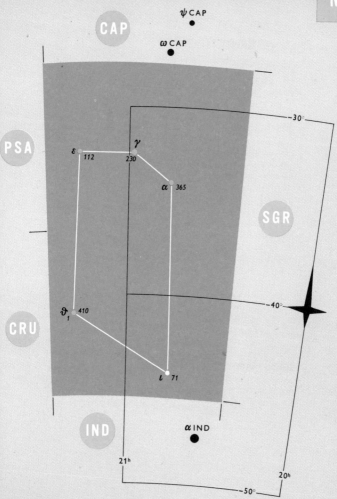

MIC

CAP

PSA

SGR

CRU

IND

ψ CAP

ω CAP

ε 112

γ 230

α 365

ϑ₁ 410

ι 71

α IND

−30°

−40°

−50°

21ʰ

20ʰ

●5 ●4 ●3

MICROSCOPIUM

MONOCEROS

Monocerotis   Mon   The Unicorn

This constellation was introduced by Johannes Hevelius in 1690. It depicts that fabulous animal having the body of a horse with a single horn in the middle of its forehead.

α **Monocerotis** is a giant, of spectral type K0, with a visual magnitude of 4.07, and an absolute magnitude 0.3. Light from this star takes 180 years to reach the Earth.

β **Monocerotis** is a triple star with two components of almost the same luminosity, namely 4.74 and 4.64, the same spectral type B3, and the same distance, 470 light years, from the Earth. The third component has a brightness of 5.6. A medium-large telescope is required for resolution.

γ **Monocerotis** is a star of magnitude 4.09 and spectral class K2, that of the giants. It lies at a distance of 250 light years and the absolute magnitude is 0.3.

δ **Monocerotis,** 180 light years away, shines as a star of magnitude 4.09. At a distance of 10 parsecs it would be as bright as a star of magnitude 0.4.

S **Monocerotis** is an irregular periodic variable ranging between magnitudes 4.2. and 4.6. The difference in brightness is easily distinguished by the naked eye.

NGC 2264 is a fairly bright open star cluster visible with the unaided eye, but better viewed with prismatic binoculars. It occupies a space as large as that of the full Moon.

NGC 2237-9 is a beautiful gaseous nebula known as the **Rosette.** It consists of delicate filaments which shine by reflected light from the radiation of very hot stars nearby.

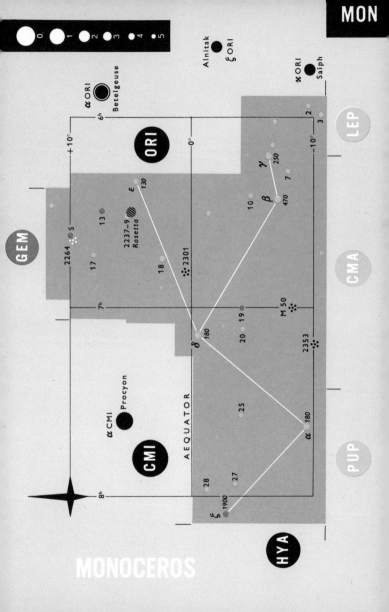

MON

MONOCEROS

MUSCA
Muscae   Mus   The Fly

Jacob Bartsch has the dubious merit of giving the name Musca to a part of the southern sky which in fact was a part of Centaurus. Musca lies between Crux and Chameleon.

α **Muscae** is a fairly bright star of magnitude 2.94 lying at a distance of 365 light years. If it were 10 parsecs away, it would be as bright as Altair, the brightest star of Aquila.

β **Muscae,** 270 light years distant, shines as a star of magnitude 3.26. The spectrum B3 ranks it among the helium stars. The absolute magnitude is −1.3.

γ **Muscae** is of spectral group B5; the distance from the Earth is also 270 light years. The absolute magnitude is −0.6.

δ **Muscae** is a hydrogen type star, of spectrum K2, and magnitude 3.63, lying at a distance of 155 light years. The absolute magnitude is 0.2.

λ **Muscae** is a star of magnitude 3.80 belonging to the group of hydrogen stars which emit white light.

η **Muscae,** lying in the immediate vicinity of the preceding star, is a red star of spectral type M2. It has a stellar magnitude of 4.71 at a distance of 410 light years. If it were 10 parsecs away, it would be as bright as β Centauri to a terrestrial observer.

●5 ●4 ●3 ●2 ●1

β CEN

−60°

CRU

CEN

α CRU

CEN

CIR

μ
λ

η

β 270

ε
80

410

α 365

−70°

δ 155

γ 270

APS

ι₁

CAR

CHA

14ʰ

13ʰ

12ʰ

−80°

MUSCA

NORMA

Normae   Nor   The Level

This constellation bears testimony to de La Caille's lack of imagination when he gave such a prosaic name to this part of the heavens near the brightest star of Centaurus. In fact Norma lies on the very edge of a dark wedge in the Milky Way. Four stars delineate the characteristic trapezium shape of the constellation.

γ_2 **Normae** is a yellow star of spectral class G8 shining from its distance of 82 light years as a star of magnitude 4.14. The absolute magnitude is 2.1.

γ_1 **Normae** is a yellow super-giant, spectral type G4, with an apparent brightness of the 5th magnitude. It lies near the foregoing star, thus making it appear a double star.

δ **Normae** is a hydrogen star of spectral type A3 with a high temperature of 10,000°K. Light from this star takes 230 years to reach the Earth. The apparent brightness is 4.84, and the absolute magnitude is 0.6.

ε **Normae,** 650 light years away, appears as a star of magnitude 4.80. The spectral type is B5; the absolute magnitude is -1.7.

η **Normae** is a yellow star of spectral class G4 lying at a distance of 190 light years. It is seen from the Earth as a star of magnitude 4.74. At a distance of 10 parsecs, the brightness would be 0.9.

The region around Norma is rich in stars because the southern part of this constellation lies in the Milky Way.

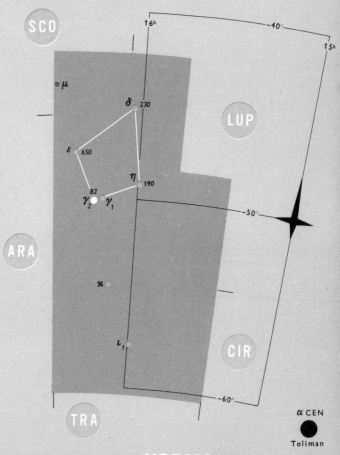

●5 ●4 ●3 ●2 ●1 ●0

SCO

μ

δ 230

ε 650

η 190

82
γ₂ γ₁

LUP

16ʰ

−40°

15ʰ

−50°

ARA

ϰ

ι₁

−60°

CIR

TRA

α CEN
Toliman

NORMA

OCTANS

Octantis   Oct   The Octant

This is a constellation which by virtue of its location at the south celestial pole should be of the same importance to sailors as Ursa Minor in the northern sky. This, however, is not the case because of the faintness of the stars which it contains. It lacks an outstanding bright star such as Polaris. σ Octantis, the star nearest to the south celestial pole, has a magnitude of 5.5., which is insufficient for purposes of navigation. Sailors therefore set their course by another celestial object to which reference is made on page 250. Octans comprises the following stars:

α **Octantis** is an exception to the rule that α, the first letter of the Greek alphabet, is used to denote the brightest star of a constellation. The apparent visual magnitude is 5.24, the distance from the Earth is 148 light years, and the spectral class is F4.

β **Octantis** is a star of which all that is known is that it has an apparent magnitude of 4.34 and belongs to the spectral class F1. The absolute magnitude is not definitely known.

δ **Octantis,** lying at a distance of 205 light years, shines as a star of magnitude 4.14. The absolute magnitude is 0.2; the spectrum is K2.

ε **Octantis** is a faint red star of spectral type M6, which lies near β Octantis.

ϑ **Octantis,** 250 light years away, is seen by a terrestrial observer as a star of magnitude 4.73. The spectrum K5 is that of orange stars. At a distance of 10 parsecs it would have the brightness of a star of magnitude 0.3.

ν **Octantis,** spectrum K0, is the brightest of the group. It lies at a distance of 84 light years, and is seen by a terrestrial observer as a star of magnitude 3.74. The absolute magnitude is 1.7.

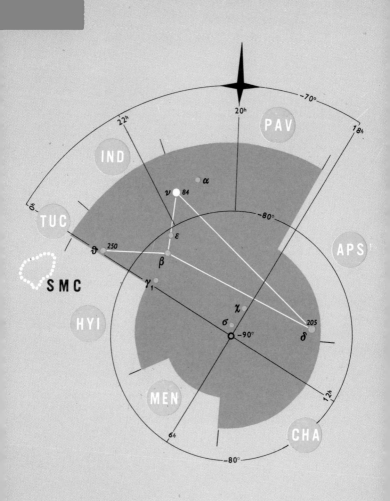

OCTANS

OPHIUCHUS

Ophiuchi   Oph   The Serpent Holder

Ophiuchus is a constellation made up of three parts: the serpent's head in the west, the serpent holder in the middle, and the serpent's tail in the east. It is perhaps supposed to represent Aesculapius, the Greek god of medicine.

α **Ophiuchi,** or **Ras Alhague,** from the Arabic for 'head of the serpent-charmer', is a bright white star of approximate magnitude 2.04 lying at a distance of 60 light years. It belongs to the group of hydrogen stars with an effective surface temperature of 10,000°K. An interesting feature of the spectrum is provided by the dark lines caused by interstellar gas between the star and Earth, perhaps part of an extensive calcium envelope of that star.

β **Ophiuchi,** or **Kelb Alrai** (Cebalrai), is a giant star of spectral type K1. Lying at a distance of 125 light years, it has an apparent brightness of 2.94. The absolute magnitude is 0.1.

η **Ophiuchi,** or **Sabik,** meaning 'preceding', is a double star of apparent magnitudes 3.2 and 3.5. The period of revolution is 80 years. Both components are of spectral type A2. The distance from the Earth is 73 light years.

ϱ **Ophiuchi** is a system of four stars of magnitudes 5.2, 5.9, 6.6, and 7.1, lying at a distance of 410 light years.

M 10, M 12 and **M 19** are bright globular star clusters.

Velox Barnardi. This 9th magnitude star discovered by the American astronomer E. E. Barnard, is an exception to the rules of selection for this atlas. It has the largest proper motion discovered to date; the star moves annually a distance of 10.25 seconds of arc across the celestial sphere. It is one of the closest stars to the Earth, being only 6 light years away.

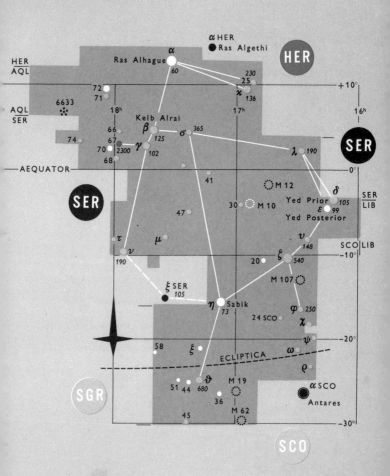

•5 •4 •3 •2 •1

α HER
● Ras Algethi

α
Ras Alhague
60

HER

HER
AQL

+10°

16h

72
71

25

230

κ
136

AQL
SER

6633

18h

Kelb Alrai

β
125

σ
365

17h

λ 190

SER

66
67
70
68

2300

γ
102

AEQUATOR

0°

41

SER
LIB

M 12

δ
105

74

SER

30

M 10

Yed Prior
ε 99
Yed Posterior

47

μ

ν
148

SCO LIB

τ
ν
190

20

ξ
540

-10°

M 107

ξ SER
105

η Sabik
73

φ 250

24 SCO

χ

ψ

58

ξ

ω

ECLIPTICA

-20°

ρ

SGR

51 44
45

ϑ
680

36

M 19

M 62

α SCO
Antares

-30°

SCO

OPHIUCHUS

ORION

Orionis   Ori   Orion

In the XIth Book of the Odyssey, Homer speaks of Orion as the lover of the rose-fingered Aurora. The constellation comprises the following important stars:

α **Orionis,** or **Betelgeuse,** from *ibt al jauzah* meaning 'armpit of the central one', is a super-giant with a diameter 300—400 times that of the Sun. The spectrum is M2 and therefore it is red. The surface temperature is about 3000°K. Betelgeuse is a variable star, but with a range that cannot be discerned by the untrained eye. Its distance from the Earth is 470 light years.

β **Orionis,** or **Rigel,** from the Arabic for 'giant's leg', is in fact a complex system of five stars. The visual magnitude is 0.34, the absolute magnitude is −8.2 and the distance from the Earth is 1300 light years.

γ **Orionis,** or **Bellatrix,** is another super-giant of spectral type B2, 325 light years away. To a terrestrial observer it appears as a 1.70 magnitude star; though from a distance of 10 parsecs it would be as bright as Antares in Scorpius.

δ **Orionis,** or **Mintaka,** 'giant's belt', is a multiple star system of five stars revolving about a common centre. The spectrum of the primary is that of a rare type of star with temperatures up to 35,000°K. The apparent magnitude is 2.48; the absolute magnitude is −6.0. The distance from the Earth, as in the case of many other stars in Orion, is 1300 light years.

ε **Orionis,** or **Alnilam,** is the central star in Orion's Belt. Its apparent magnitude is 1.75, and it belongs to spectral group B0. The absolute magnitude is −7.0. Its distance from the Earth is 1300 light years.

ζ **Orionis,** or **Alnitak,** lies in Orion's Belt. It is 1300 light years distant and its apparent magnitude is 2.05. The absolute brightness is −6.4.

κ **Orionis,** or **Saiph,** is a super-giant of spectral group B0, the helium stars, lying at a distance of 1300 light years. The visual magnitude is 2.20; the absolute magnitude is −6.7.

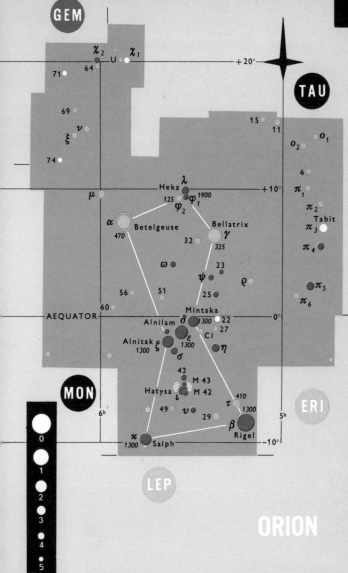

ORI

GEM

+20°

χ₂   χ₁
  U
64
71

TAU

69
ν
ξ
74

15
11

o₂   o₁

6
π₁
π₂

Tabit
π₃
π₄

+10°
μ   Heka λ
              125 φ₁ 1900
          φ₂

α Betelgeuse   Bellatrix
470   γ
           32   325

ω   23
           ψ   ρ
56   51   25

π₅
π₆

60

AEQUATOR   Mintaka   0°
          Alnilam δ 1300
                        22
          ε   27
Alnitak ζ   CI
1300   η
          σ

              42
Hatysa ι   M 43
              M 42
  49   υ 29
MON   τ 410
6ʰ   β 1300
5ʰ   Rigel
κ   Saiph   -10°
1300

ERI

LEP

ORION

0
1
2
3
4
5

PAVO

Pavonis   Pav   The Peacock

This constellation was depicted by Bayer in his *Uranometria*.

α **Pavonis,** or **Peacock,** the brightest of the group, lies almost on the boundary of Indus and Telescopium at a distance of 230 light years; it shines as a star of magnitude 2.12. The absolute magnitude is −2.3.

β **Pavonis** is a helium type star of 3.60 stellar magnitude with a temperature of about 10,000°K. It is 112 light years away. At a distance of 10 parsecs it would be as bright as Achernar.

γ **Pavonis** is a yellowish star, spectral type F8, with a brightness of 4.30. Light from this star takes 29 years to reach the Earth.

δ **Pavonis** is a dwarf star, spectral type G4, with an apparent visual magnitude of 3.64, lying at a distance of 19 light years.

ε **Pavonis** shines as a star of magnitude 4.10 at a distance of 270 light years. The spectral type is A0, where calcium, hydrogen and metallic lines begin to appear.

ζ **Pavonis** is a 4.10 magnitude star, orange in colour, spectral type K0, lying at a distance of 109 light years. The absolute magnitude is 1.5.

η **Pavonis** is a type K1 star with effective temperature of about 4500°K. A terrestrial observer sees it as a star of magnitude 3.58; but at a distance of 10 parsecs it would be about as bright as Aldebaran in Taurus. Its distance from the Earth is 180 light years.

Pavo contains several star clusters of which **NGC 6752** is the brightest.

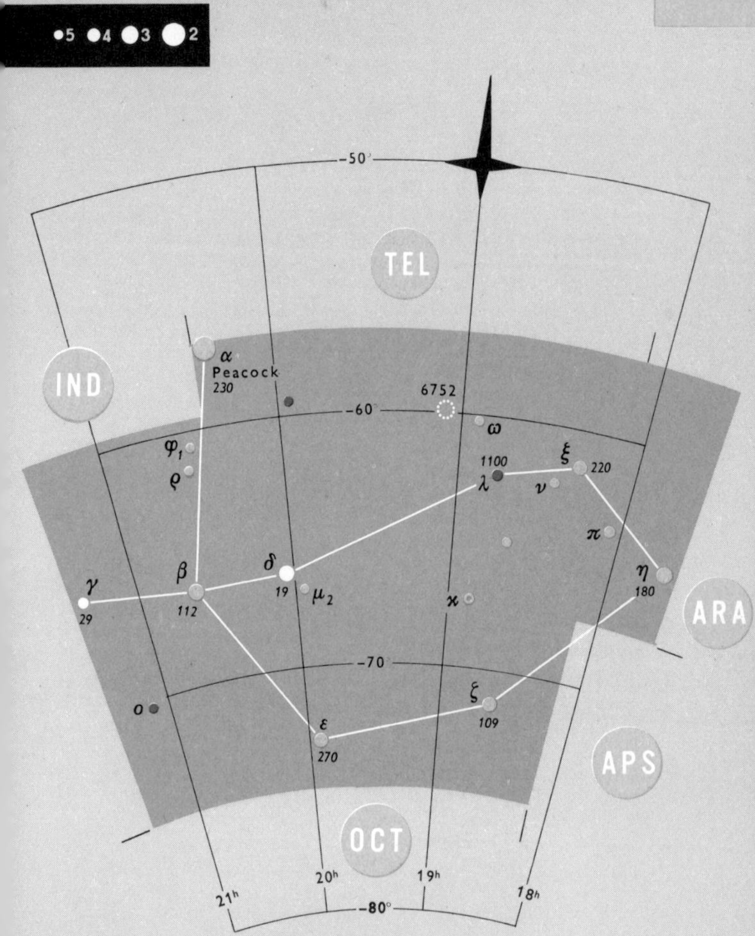
5 4 3 2
-50°
-60°
-70°
-80°
TEL
IND
ARA
APS
OCT
α
Peacock
230
6752
ω
φ1
ρ
1100
ξ
220
λ
ν
π
β
112
δ
19
μ2
γ
29
η
180
ϰ
ο
ε
270
ζ
109
21h
20h
19h
18h

PAVO

PEGASUS
Pegasi   Peg   Pegasus

According to mythology, Pegasus, the Winged Horse, was the son of Neptune and Medusa.

α **Pegasi,** or **Markab,** Arabic for 'saddle', is a star of spectral group B9. It shines as a star of magnitude 2.57; the absolute magnitude, however, is 0.1. Light from this star takes 102 years to reach the Earth.

β **Pegasi,** or **Scheat,** meaning 'shoulder', is a giant star of spectral type M2 in which the absorption bands produced by molecules and lines of metals are most intense. It lies at a distance of 172 light years and shines as a star of magnitude 2.61. The absolute magnitude is −0.1. It is a variable star ranging from magnitude 2.4. to 2.8.

γ **Pegasi,** or **Algenib** (in Bayer's atlas it denotes the horse's wing), is a star 470 light years away. The spectral class is B2, brightness 2.87. At a distance of 10 parsecs it would be as bright as a star of magnitude −2.8.

ε **Pegasi,** or **Enif,** is a super-giant 820 light years distant, which is seen from the Earth as a star of magnitude 2.54; however at a distance of 10 parsecs it would be one of the brightest stars in the sky. The K2 spectrum features a large number of metallic lines. The temperature of the star is approximately 4500°K.

ζ **Pegasi,** or **Homam,** 180 light years away, shines as a star of magnitude 3.61. The absolute magnitude is −0.1. It belongs to spectral class B8, the so-called helium stars with a high temperature of about 20,000°K.

η **Pegasi,** or **Matar,** is a yellow giant of spectral type G2, lying at a distance of 230 light years. The apparent magnitude is 3.10. The absolute brightness at 10 parsecs would equal that of a star of magnitude −0.2.

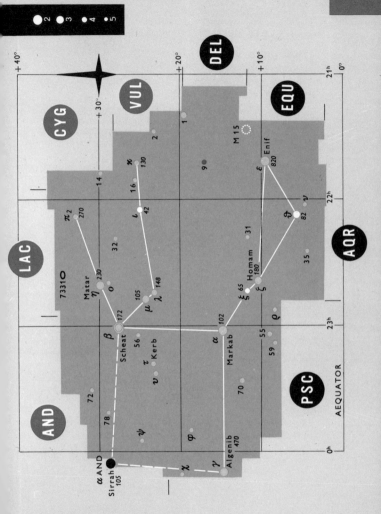

PEGASUS

PERSEUS

Persei   Per   Perseus

According to Sophocles, Perseus, the son of Zeus and Danae, slew Medusa and rescued Andromeda.

α **Persei,** or **Algenib** (meaning 'side'), or **Mirfak** (meaning 'elbow'). This star is a super-giant of spectral type F5 with an apparent brightness of 1.90 lying at a distance of 470 light years. At a distance of 10 parsecs it would be as bright as Sirius.

β **Persei,** or **Algol,** meaning 'demon', is an eclipsing variable comprising two components ranging between magnitude 2.2 and 3.5 in a period of approximately 2.87 days; the eclipse lasts 10 hours. Its distance from the Earth is 82 light years.

γ **Persei** is a giant of spectral class F7 + A3 with a surface temperature of approximately 7500°K. Lying at a distance of 205 light years it has an apparent magnitude of 3.08. The absolute brightness is −0.9.

ε **Persei,** 1100 light years away, shines with an apparent magnitude of 2.96. It belongs to spectral group B1, the group of helium stars. At a distance of 10 parsecs it would be twice as bright as Sirius.

ζ **Persei,** or **Menkhib** (in *Uranometria* this star marks the leg of Perseus), is a super-giant of spectral class B1 with an effective surface temperature of about 20,000°K. Lying at a distance of 820 light years it shines as a star of magnitude 2.91. The absolute magnitude is −5.3.

NGC 869 and **NGC 884** are two open star clusters visible to the unaided eye on clear nights. They are also designated χ and h Persei, and are together known as the **Double Cluster.**

M 34 or **NGC 1039** is an open star cluster the size of the apparent diameter of the full Moon.

Amongst the stars lies the gaseous nebula **NGC 1490,** also called the **California Nebula** for its resemblance to the contours of that state. Before that it was known as the **Dragon Nebula.**

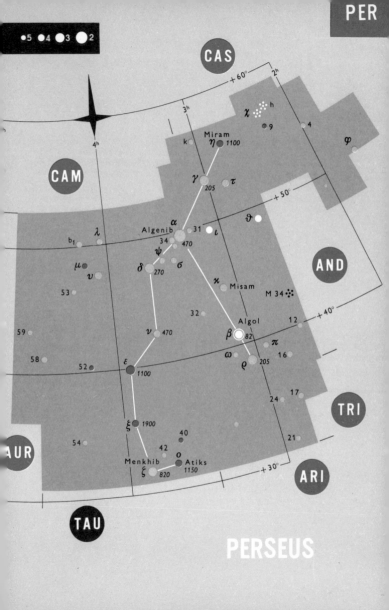

PER

●5 ●4 ●3 ●2

CAS

+60°   2ʰ

3ʰ   χ   h
                                    9   4

4ʰ   k   Miram
                     η ● 1100   φ

CAM   γ ●   τ   +50°
                     205

AND

λ   Algenib α   31
b₁   34   ι   ϑ
μ   ψ
   ν   δ ●   σ
53   270
                                    κ
                              32   Misam   M 34

CAS   Algol   12
59   ν ● 470   β ●
                                           82
58   ω   ρ   π   16
        52 ●   ε ●   205
                1100   24   17

54   ξ ● 1900
                          40
                     42   21
        Menkhib ζ ●   o Atiks
                 820   1150

                              +30°

TAU   ARI

PERSEUS

CAM

AUR

TRI

PHOENIX

Phoenicis   Phe   The Phoenix

East of the bright star Achernar lies the constellation shown on stellar maps as the Phoenix. It was introduced in 1603 by Bayer in his *Uranometria*.

α **Phoenicis** is a fairly bright star, belonging to spectral class G5, close to that of our Sun. Light from this star takes 76 years to reach the Earth. The apparent magnitude is 2.44; at a distance of 10 parsecs the brightness would be 0.6.

β **Phoenicis** is somewhat less bright, having an apparent magnitude of 3.35, but belongs to the same group of yellow stars — its spectral type is G4. It lies at a distance of 180 light years, the absolute magnitude is −0.4.

γ **Phoenicis** is a red star of spectral type M1, 1400 light years away. The terrestrial observer sees it as a star of magnitude 3.40; the absolute magnitude is −5.0.

δ **Phoenicis,** stellar magnitude 3.96, is a yellow star, type G4, lying at a distance of 120 light years. The absolute magnitude is 1.1.

κ **Phoenicis** is a hydrogen star of spectral type A3, and apparent magnitude 3.90, 49 light years distant. The absolute magnitude is 3.0.

Phoenix contains no other bright objects such as galaxies and star clusters. The constellation lies outside the Milky Way.

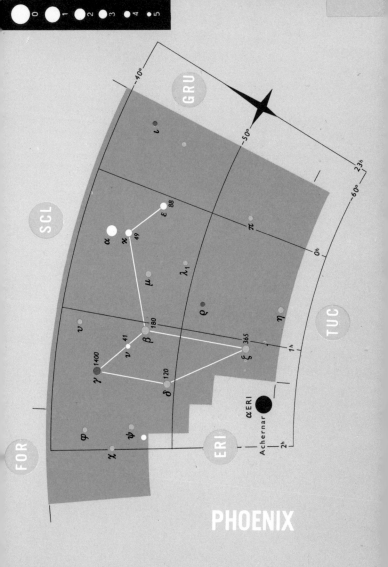

PHOENIX

PICTOR

Pictoris   Pic   The Painter's Easel

Equuleus Pictoris (Painter's Easel) was the name originally given to this constellation by Abbé de La Caille. The International Astronomical Union, however, adopted the name Pictor, meaning painter. This constellation lies east of Carina with its bright star Canopus and contains the following three stars:

α **Pictoris,** belonging to the group of hydrogen stars, which are white and have an effective temperature of about 10,000°K.

β **Pictoris,** belonging to the same spectral group, is 56 light years away. The apparent magnitude is 3.94.

γ **Pictoris** is an orange star of spectral class K1. Lying at a distance of 220 light years it glows as a star of magnitude 4.38.

Pictor is not rich in bright objects. A telescope, however, reveals a number of faint stars and galaxies, and photography shows up even fainter objects. More detailed study is possible with radiotelescopes which show that this constellation is a source of radiation having a frequency of 18.3 Mc/s.

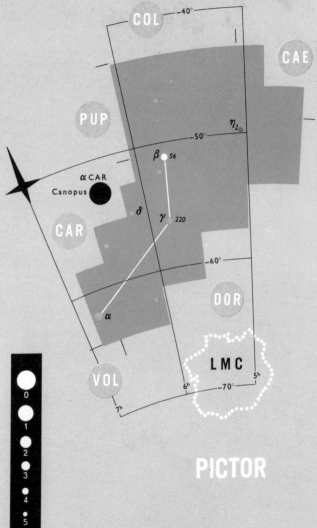

PIC

COL
−40°

CAE

PUP

η₂

−50°

β 56

α CAR
Canopus

δ

γ 220

CAR

−60°

DOR

α

VOL

6ʰ
−70°

5ʰ

7ʰ

LMC

PICTOR

0
1
2
3
4
5

PISCES

Piscium   Psc   The Fishes

One of the fishes lies near Mirach in Andromeda, the second
below the Square of Pegasus. The myth about this constellation dates back to the period of Syrian culture, and it is
referred to by Ovid. The Roman version is that Venus
transformed herself and her son Cupid into fishes to escape
the wrathful Typhon in the battle of the giants.

α **Piscium,** or **Alrisha** (Al Rischa), from the Arabic for
'cord', is a very close double, the two components revolving
about a common centre in a period of 720 years. Both belong
to spectral group A2, i.e. the hydrogen stars. The brighter
component has a magnitude of 4.33, the other a magnitude
of 5.23. Light from this double star takes 130 years to reach
the Earth. The absolute magnitude is 1.3.

β **Piscium** glows as a star of magnitude 4.52 at its
distance of 325 light years. The spectrum B5 places it among
the helium stars with estimated surface temperature of
20,000°K. At a distance of 10 parsecs it would be as bright
as a star of magnitude −0.4.

γ **Piscium** is a yellow giant of spectral type G5 125 light
years distant, shining with an apparent magnitude of 3.85.
At a distance of 10 parsecs it would be as bright as Achernar
in Eridanus.

ι **Piscium** is a dwarf star, spectral type F5, apparent
magnitude 4.28, 48 light years away. At a distance of 10
parsecs it would be only slightly brighter, like a star of
magnitude 3.4.

TV Piscium is a semi-regular variable star with amplitude ranging between magnitudes 4.6 and 5.2 in a period of
49 days. The distance from the Earth is 325 light years.

30 Piscium is a sub-giant of the M3 spectral group of red
stars. 235 light years away it has an apparent magnitude
of 4.66.

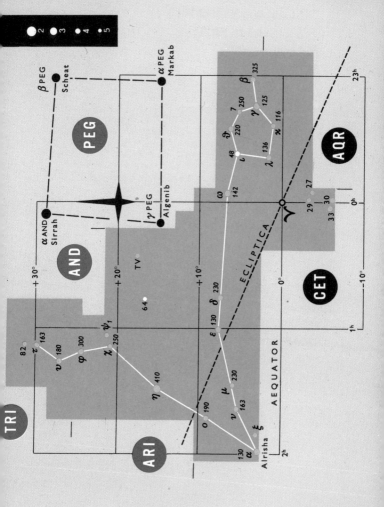

PISCES

PISCIS AUSTRINUS or
PISCIS AUSTRALIS

Piscis Austrini or
Piscis Australis   PsA   The Southern Fish

In Europe at midnight in the month of August or in the evening hours of October, the bright star Fomalhaut can be seen on the southern horizon. This star is part of the constellation known as the Southern Fish ever since the days when the cult of the Egyptian goddess Isis was widespread among the Greeks and later among the Romans. It is linked with the legend that the goddess was saved by a fish.

α **Piscis Austrini,** or **Fomalhaut,** from the Arabic for 'mouth of the fish', is a star with a surface temperature of about 9000°K, belonging to spectral class A2. It shines as a star of magnitude 1.29 at a distance of about 23 light years.

β **Piscis Austrini** is also a hydrogen star of spectral type A0 lying at a distance of 220 light years. The apparent magnitude is 4.36; the absolute magnitude is 0.2.

γ **Piscis Austrini** is a red giant of spectral type A0, 180 light years distant from the Earth. The apparent magnitude is 4.52; the absolute magnitude is 0.8.

ε **Piscis Austrini,** 250 light years away, appears to the terrestrial observer to have a magnitude of 4.22. The absolute magnitude is 0.2. The spectrum B8 ranges it among the helium stars with an effective surface temperature of about 20,000°K.

PSA

●5 ●4 ●3 ●2 ●1

CET

CAP

—20°

ε 250

Fomalhaut

α

23

—30°

ϑ

δ 180

β 220

τ

γ 180

μ 125

ι 93

υ

CL

π

MIC

23h

22h

GRU

—40°

PISCIS AUSTRINUS

PUPPIS

Puppis   Pup   The Stern

The Stern is part of the former constellation Argo Navis (the Ship Argo).

α **Puppis** is a yellowish star of magnitude 3.76, the spectrum resembling that of our Sun. It is 142 light years distant and the absolute magnitude is 0.6.

ζ **Puppis,** or **Naos,** (the meaning is unknown) is 1100 light years away and appears to have a magnitude of 2.27. ξ Puppis is a very hot star with an effective temperature of about 35,000°K. The spectrum O5 has intense absorption lines produced by ionized helium. This type of star is very rare.

L₂L₁ Puppis is an optical double. The brighter component is 540 light years distant and has a magnitude of 5.04, the other is a variable star ranging from magnitude 3.4 to 6.2 in a period of 140.5 days. The first star is of spectral type A0, the second M5. L₂ Puppis is 180 light years distant.

ν **Puppis** is a star of magnitude 3.18, spectral group B0, lying at a distance of 142 light years.

ξ **Puppis,** or **Azmidiske,** (the meaning is unknown) 1100 light years away, has an apparent magnitude of 3.47. It is a yellow super-giant; and if it were located at a distance of 32.6 light years it would be as bright as the planet Venus.

π **Puppis** is 230 light years distant, and it appears to a terrestrial observer to have a brightness of 2.74. The spectrum K5 indicates that it is a star with lower surface temperature than that of the Sun. The absolute magnitude is −1.5.

τ **Puppis,** 130 light years away, has an apparent magnitude of 2.83.

Puppis contains a number of open star clusters of which **M 47** or **NGC 2422** is the most beautiful.

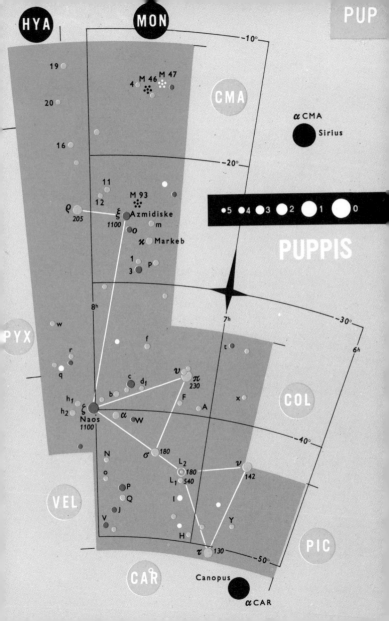

PYXIS
Pyxidis Pyx The Mariner's Compass

As the name indicates this constellation is part of the ship Argo, which in the new astronomical nomenclature was subdivided into several parts. Pyxis is abbreviated from Pyxis Nautica, which is Latin for 'nautical box' or 'compass'. The following several faint stars delineate this instrument in the sky.

α **Pyxidis** has a spectrum characteristic of helium stars with a high temperature of about 20,000°K. Lying at a distance of 470 light years α Pyxidis has the brightness of a star of magnitude 2.01. At a distance of 10 parsecs it would be brighter than Fomalhaut in Piscis Australis.

β **Pyxidis** is a solar type star with an apparent brightness of 4.04, lying at a distance of 230 light years. The absolute magnitude is −2.1.

γ **Pyxidis** is a star of spectral class K4 in which the lines of metals are most intense and molecular absorption bands begin to appear. In the sky it shines as a star of magnitude 4.19 from its distance of 190 light years. At 10 parsecs its brightness would be of approximately 1st magnitude.

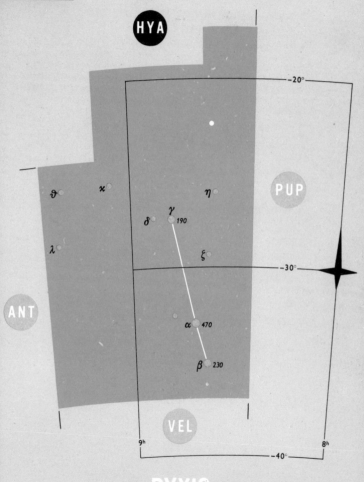

PYXIS

RETICULUM
Reticuli   Ret   The Net

By introducing this constellation de La Caille wished to memorialize that important instrument of astronomers, the reticule, used by them in measuring the positions of stars. Reticulum contains a group of faint stars resembling the small constellation Delphinus in the northern sky. They are easily located, for they lie in the proximity of the Large Magellanic Cloud.

α **Reticuli** is a star of magnitude 3.36, of spectral class G5 and effective temperature somewhat lower than that of the Sun. The estimated distance from the Earth is 365 light years.

β **Reticuli,** 76 light years away, is a red star of spectral class G9. This type of star has a lower surface temperature of about 6500°K.

γ **Reticuli** also belongs to spectral class M5. Stars of this type are not very common, comprising only about 7 per cent of the total number in the sky. γ Reticuli has an apparent magnitude of 4.46.

ε **Reticuli,** 80 light years distant, shines as a star of magnitude 4.42. It is a sub-giant of spectral class K5, a type of star which is cooler than our Sun. The absolute magnitude is 2.5.

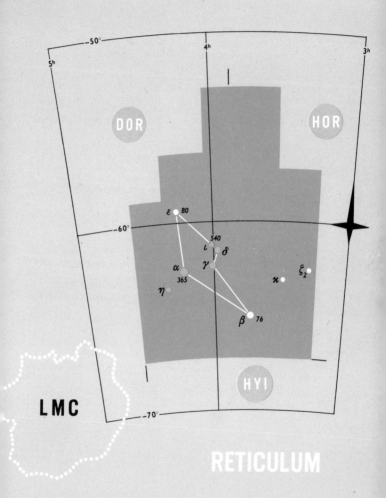

DOR

HOR

ε 80

540
ι
δ
α γ
365
η

x ξ₂

β 76

HYI

LMC

RETICULUM

SAGITTA
Sagittae   Sge   The Arrow

In the middle of the Milky Way above the star Altair in Aquila, lies the ancient constellation the Arrow. The Greeks knew it under the name of Toxon or Oistos, and it was the Romans who gave it the Latin name Sagitta; the Arab term for it was Al Sahm. According to one of many legends Sagitta is a reminder of Hercules' fight with the eagle which at Vulcan's orders daily gouged the liver from the body of Prometheus chained to a rock in the Caucasus Mountains. Sagitta is best viewed in the mountains on clear moonless nights.

α **Sagittae,** or **Sham,** though shining like a star of magnitude 4.37, is in reality a super-giant of spectral class F8, in which the hydrogen lines weaken and the calcium and other metallic lines increase. The temperature of these stars is about 7500°K. The estimated distance is 540 light years; the absolute brightness is −1.7.

β **Sagittae** belongs to spectral group G7, which is similar to that of our Sun (G2). The temperature falls to 6000°K. Stars of this group are yellow and comprise about 16 per cent of all stars in the sky. β Sagittae has an apparent magnitude of 4.45 and an absolute magnitude of 0.0. It lies at a distance of 250 light years.

γ **Sagittae** is a giant of spectral type M0 which comprises stars with a relatively low surface temperature of about 3500°K; it is therefore red in colour. The distance from the Earth is 190 light years; the apparent magnitude is 3.71, and the absolute magnitude is −0.1.

δ **Sagittae** is a giant with a composite spectrum, type M2 and A0. It is 410 light years distant from the Earth and is seen as a star of magnitude 3.78. The absolute magnitude is −1.7.

Sagitta contains one bright open star cluster **NGC 6838** close to ζ Sagittae, a triple star outside the scope of this atlas.

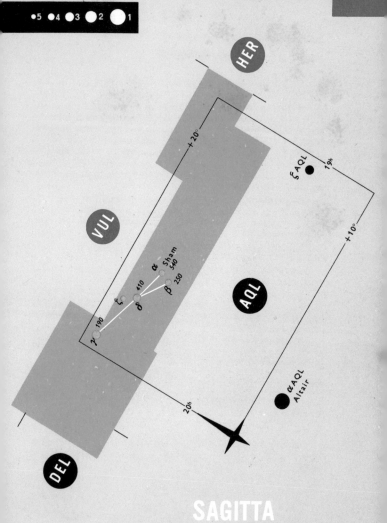

SGE

HER

ζ AQL   19ʰ

VUL

α   Sham
        540
   ζ   410
      δ   β   250

AQL

γ   190

DEL

α AQL
Altair

+20

+10°

20ʰ

SAGITTA

•5 •4 •3 ●2 ◯1

SAGITTARIUS

Sagittarii   Sgr   The Archer

This constellation is the ninth sign of the zodiac and in older atlases was depicted as a centaur holding a bow and arrow.

α **Sagittarii, Rukbat** (knee) or **Alrami** (the archer). This is a star of magnitude 4.11 and was mistakenly designated as α. It lies at a distance of 250 light years. Spectral type B9.

δ **Sagittarii,** or **Kaus Medius** (Kaus Meridionalis), denotes the mid-arc of the bow. This star is a giant of spectral type K2, 112 light years away. Apparent magnitude 2.84, absolute magnitude 0.1.

ε **Sagittarii,** or **Kaus Australis,** the southern part of the bow, is a sub-giant of spectral class B9. 136 light years away it shines as a star of magnitude 1.95. The absolute magnitude is −1.3.

λ **Sagittarii,** or **Kaus Borealis,** the northern part of the bow, has an apparent magnitude of 2.94. In reality it is a giant of spectral class K1 lying at a distance of 84 light years. The absolute brightness is 0.9.

σ **Sagittarii,** or **Nunki,** is a star of spectral type B3, lying 180 light years distant from the Earth. The apparent magnitude is 2.14; the absolute magnitude is −1.6.

Of the open star clusters in this constellation the following, listed under their Messier numbers, are the brightest: **M 23, M 24** and **M 25.**

Near the galactic centre of the constellation are several spectacular gaseous nebulae. The following are frequently mentioned in astronomical literature: **M 20** or **NGC 6514,** the famous **Trifid Nebula; M 8** or **NGC 6523,** the **Lagoon Nebula;** and **M 17** or **NGC 6618,** the **Omega Nebula.**

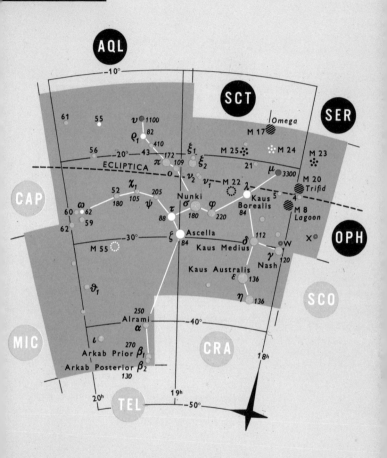

•5 •4 •3 •2

AQL

SCT

SER

CAP

OPH

SCO

MIC

CRA

SCR

TEL

61   55   υ 1100
            ϱ₁ 82
                410
56   43   172
—20°— ECLIPTICA   π 109   o
                    ν₂   ν₁ — M 22
52 χ₁   205   Nunki   φ
  105   σ
   ω   180   ψ τ   180   220
60 62   88
   59   ξ   Ascella
62   84   Kaus Medius
      M 55   δ   112
      —30°—   Kaus Australis   γ
                    ε   136
   ϑ₁   η   136

Omega
M 17
M 25   M 24   M 23
ξ₁
ξ₂   21   μ 3300
      λ   M 20
      5   Trifid
   Kaus   4
   Borealis   M 8
   84   Lagoon
      W   X
      120
   Nash

250
Alrami
  α
ι
270
Arkab Prior β₁
Arkab Posterior β₂
   130

—10°—

—40°—

18h

20h   19h   —50°—

SAGITTARIUS

SCORPIUS

Scorpii   Sco   The Scorpion

α **Scorpii,** or **Antares,** is a red super-giant, its diameter being 300 times that of the Sun. It belongs to spectral class M1 and has a relatively low surface temperature of about 3500°K. Circling around it is a companion with a much higher temperature and twice the size of the Sun. According to Dr W. Campbell it moves in the hydrogen atmosphere of the primary. Antares is 365 light years distant from the Earth; the absolute magnitude is −5.0.

$β_1, β_2$ **Scorpii,** or **Acrab,** is the name for the front part of the Scorpion. Acrab comprises two hot suns. The brighter of the two has a companion which was revealed by spectroscopy. The system is 540 light years away. Viewed from the Earth, Acrab has a brightness of 2.90; the absolute magnitude is −3.4.

δ **Scorpii,** or **Dschubba,** meaning 'scorpion's brain', is a sub-giant of spectral class B0, lying at a distance of 990 light years.

λ **Scorpii,** or **Shaula,** from the Arabic for 'scorpion's sting'. At 10 parsecs it would shine like a star of magnitude −3.0, but as it lies at a distance of 270 light years it is seen by a terrestrial observer as a star of magnitude 1.71. The star's B2 spectrum has revealed the presence of a smaller companion revolving aroung the former in a period of 5.6 days.

σ **Scorpii** is a variable star of the same type as β Canis Majoris with amplitude ranging from 3.0 to 3.8 in a period of 0.247 days. It is a helium star of spectral type B1. The distance from the Earth is 630 light years.

Among the brightest objects in Scorpius are: **M 6** or **NGC 6405** and **M 7** or **NGC 6475**, both open clusters visible with a small telescope; the globular clusters **M 4** or **NGC 6121**, **M 80** or **NGC 6093**; and the open cluster **NGC 6322.**

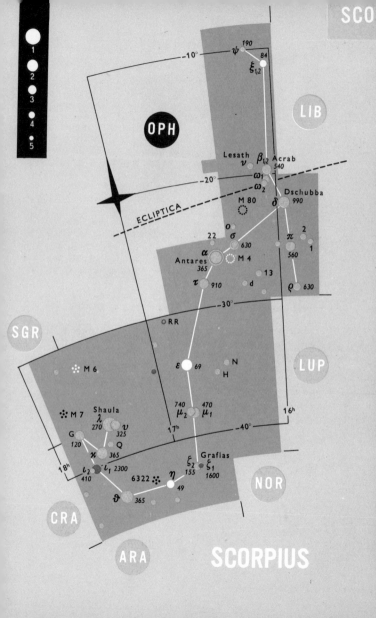

SCULPTOR

Sculptoris   Scl   The Sculptor

Sculptor is a constellation which de La Caille originally called the Sculptor's Workshop but it is now generally called the Sculptor. It lies west of Fomalhaut, the bright star in Piscis Australis.

α **Sculptoris** has an apparent visual magnitude of 4.39 at a distance of 270 light years. At a distance of 10 parsecs it would be as bright as Arcturus in Boötes. It is a helium star of spectral type B5 lying between Phoenix and Cetus.

β **Sculptoris** is somewhat closer than α Scl. It is 250 light years distant, and appears to the terrestrial observer as a star of magnitude 4.46. The absolute magnitude is 0.0, the spectral type B9 with an effective temperature of about 15,000°K.

γ **Sculptoris** is a yellow sub-giant, spectral type G8, and its physical characteristics are similar to those of the Sun. 155 light years away it shines as a star of magnitude 4.51. The absolute magnitude is 1.1.

δ **Sculptoris,** 163 light years distant, has an apparent magnitude of 4.64. It is a helium star, of spectral type A0. The absolute magnitude is 1.0.

NGC 253 is an extragalactic nebula with a total brightness of 7th magnitude, and it is therefore visible with binoculars.

Sculptor, like Fornax, contains a cluster of galaxies relatively close to the Milky Way, even though they are three times further away than the Magellanic Clouds.

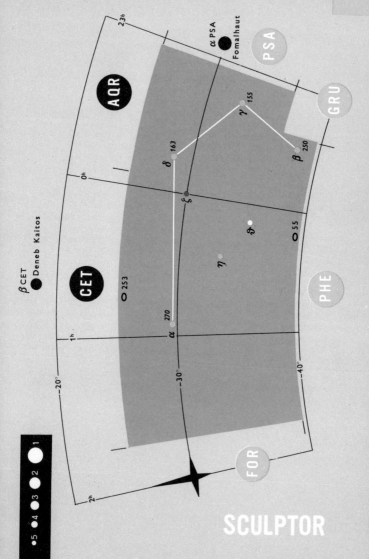

SCL

SCULPTOR

SCUTUM
Scuti   Sct   The Shield

Scutum is an inconspicuous constellation which attracts attention only because of the rich background of the Milky Way. On summer nights it can be seen between Aquila and Sagittarius. The original name of this constellation, given it by Hevelius in his *Firmamentum Sobieskianum* (1690) was Sobiesky's Shield, in honour of the Polish count who aided Hevelius when his observatory in Danzig burned to the ground.

α **Scuti** is a stellar giant of spectral group K5 with a surface temperature much lower than that of the Sun. Lying at a distance of 205 light years it has an apparent magnitude of 4.06.

β **Scuti** is a yellow super-giant of spectral type G7, appearing to a terrestrial observer as a star of magnitude 4.47. If it were 10 parsecs distant it would be brighter than Antares in Scorpius. The actual distance is 1300 light years.

γ **Scuti** is a typical blue star of spectral type A3, lying at a distance of 148 light years. The apparent visual magnitude is 4.73; the absolute magnitude is 1.4.

δ **Scuti,** 190 light years away, belongs to spectral class F4 with surface temperature 7500°K. It is a variable star ranging from magnitude 4.9 to 5.2 in a period of 0.194 days.

ζ **Scuti** is an orange giant of spectral group K0 lying at a distance of 230 light years.

Scutum contains several interesting star clusters, one of which is **M 11**, an open star cluster resolvable with opera glasses. The stars are spaced over an area about one-third the size of the full Moon.

●5 ●4 ◯3

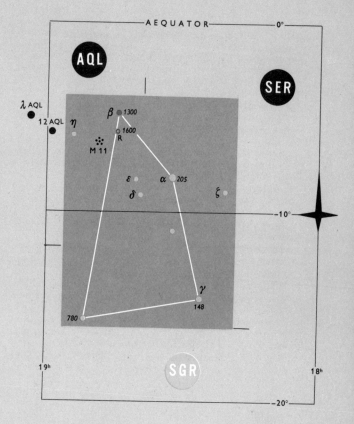

AEQUATOR 0°

AQL

SER

λ AQL

12 AQL   η

β ● 1300

R ◯ 1600

M 11

ε   α ● 205

δ   ξ

-10°

γ

148

780

19ʰ   SGR   18ʰ

-20°

SCUTUM

SERPENS — CAPUT AND CAUDA

Serpentis   Ser   The Serpent

Caput (head) and Cauda (tail) are two separate parts of the constellation Serpens.

CAPUT: α **Serpentis,** or **Unuk Elhaia** (Unuk al hay), meaning 'serpent's neck', is the brightest star in Serpens Caput. About 82 light years distant, this giant belongs to spectral group K2 with a lower surface temperature than that of the Sun. It has an apparent magnitude of 2.75 and an absolute magnitude of 0.8.

β **Serpentis** is a star of magnitude 3.74, 120 light years distant from the Earth. It is a hydrogen star with somewhat higher temperature than that of the Sun. The absolute brightness is 0.9.

γ **Serpentis** is a dwarf star of spectral class F5, 41 light years from the Earth. It shines as a star of magnitude 3.86. The absolute brightness is 3.3.

δ_1 δ_2 **Serpentis** is a double star of magnitudes 4.50 and 5.37 and dwarf star spectra A9 and A7. It lies at a distance of 172 light years.

ε **Serpentis** is a dwarf star of spectral group A6, 86 light years away. Its absolute brightness is 1.6.

M 5 or **NGC 5904** is one of the brightest globular star clusters.

CAUDA: η **Serpentis** is a sub-giant of spectral group G8, 68 light years distant from the Earth. The stellar magnitude is 3.42. It is slightly brighter than the other star in Serpens Cauda.

ξ **Serpentis,** 105 light years away, shines as a star of magnitude 3.64. The spectrum A5 classes it among the hydrogen stars. The absolute brightness is 1.1.

NGC 4756 is a scattered star cluster. **M 16** or **NGC 6611** is a star cluster enveloped by a nebula.

SER

SERPENS

CRB

BOO

VIR

LIB

HER

OPH

AEQUATOR

SCT

SGR

AQL

α CRB
Gemma

ι 250
ρ 300   κ   γ 163
         β 120
         41
π

+ 20°

+ 10°

0°

SERPENS CAPUT

δ 172
λ α Unuk Elhaia
   82
ε 86
36 μ
    190

M 5
5

10

15h

−10°

σ

δ OPH
105
ε OPH
99   υ OPH
     148
     ξ OPH
     540

16h

η OPH
72

ν
ο   ξ
    105

CAUDA

ξ

η 68

4756

ϑ Alya
142

ν OPH
190

SERPENS

M 16

17h

18h

−20°

19h

2
3
4
5

SEXTANS

Sextantis   Sex   The Sextant

In his book *Prodromus Astronomiae* Hevelius introduced new names for various regions in the sky. This was in 1690, when the constellations had no established, internationally-acknowledged boundaries — a state of affairs that gave rise to considerable confusion. Hence the endeavour to fill in the empty spaces in the sky with further small constellations. Thus the Sextant, an instrument Hevelius himself knew how to construct, found its way into the sky and into modern star catalogues and maps.

α **Sextantis** is a star of spectral class A0 with an apparent magnitude of 4.50. The distance from the Earth is expressed by a parallax of 0.012 seconds, which equals 270 light years. The absolute magnitude is −0.1.

β **Sextantis,** 365 light years distant, belongs to spectral group B5 and is seen by a terrestrial observer as a star of magnitude 4.95. At a distance of 10 parsecs it would be brighter than Arcturus, the brightest star in Boötes.

γ **Sextantis** is a blue star of apparent visual magnitude 5.16 and spectral group A0 lying at a distance of 230 light years. The absolute magnitude is 0.9.

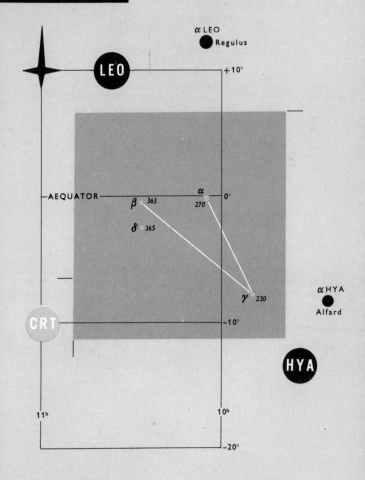

•5 •4 •3 •2 ●1

α LEO
Regulus

LEO

+10°

AEQUATOR

β 365   α
            270

δ 365

0°

γ 230

α HYA
Alfard

CRT

−10°

HYA

11ʰ   10ʰ

−20°

SEXTANS

TAURUS
Tauri   Tau   The Bull

This constellation, a reminder of the amorous adventures of Zeus, who in the form of a bull carried off the Princess Europa, is the second sign of the zodiac.

α **Tauri,** or **Aldebaran,** from the Arabic for 'follower', is a red giant with diameter 36 times that of the Sun. It lies at a distance of 64 light years. The spectral group is K5, the surface temperature is about 3000°K. The absolute magnitude is -0.6.

β **Tauti,** or **Nath,** is a giant star 142 light years away. The visual magnitude is 1.78, the absolute magnitude -1.5. In older maps this star marks one of the horns of Taurus. It is also incorporated as part of the constellation Auriga.

M 45, or **Pleiades,** is a beautiful and well-known star cluster resembling a carriage in shape. The seven stars of this cluster are spread out over a space the size of the full Moon as seen from the Earth. The whole group is enveloped in a cloud of dust and gas which is not uniformly thick at all points. Particularly conspicuous is the nebula near Merope (one of the Pleiades) which reflects the light of Merope. The brightest of the stars in the Pleiades is η **Tauri,** or **Alcyone,** a white sub-giant of spectral class B. The estimated distance of the cluster is 500 light years.

Hyades is a star cluster whose components are moving in approximately the same direction at a speed of 40 km/sec. It comprises several giants, but unlike the Pleiades has fewer bright hot stars. In all, this cluster numbers some 132 stars.

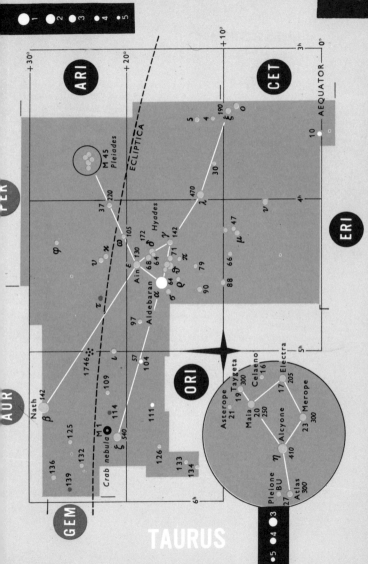

TAU

TAURUS

TELESCOPIUM
Telescopii   Tel   The Telescope

This constellation was introduced by de La Caille in honour of the invention which had such a revolutionary significance for astronomy. Telescopium is realistically depicted in the stellar atlas prepared and published in the early 19th century by Bode under the title *Uranometria Sive Astrorum Descriptio*.

α **Telescopii** is the brightest of the stars with a magnitude of 3.76 at a distance of 650 light years. The spectrum B6 shows that it belongs to the group of helium stars with an effective surface temperature of about 20,000°K. The absolute magnitude is −2.8.

δ_1 **Telescopii** is a small star of 5th magnitude the same distance from the Earth as the foregoing star. It also has a similar spectrum which reveals an otherwise invisible companion. As indicated by the index to the Greek letter there is another star in close proximity to this one which can be considered as the second component of a double star; the distance between the two, however, indicates that it is an optical double. The first is 650 light years distant, whereas the second, fainter star is much further from the Earth, namely 1088 light years.

ε **Telescopii** is a yellow star of the solar type belonging to class G5 and lying at a distance of 300 light years. The absolute magnitude is −0.2, but to a terrestrial observer it appears as a star of magnitude 4.60.

ξ **Telescopii,** 365 light years away, has a spectrum K0 characteristic of the cooler orange stars. The apparent magnitude is 4.14; the absolute magnitude is 0.8.

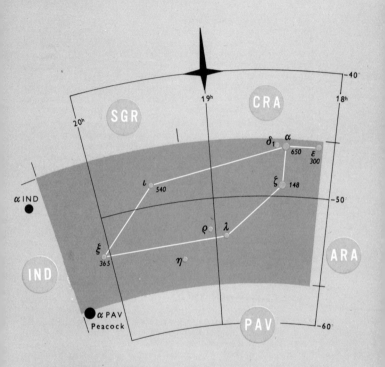

●5 ●4 ●3 ●2

TEL

CRA

SGR

19h

18h

20h

δ₁   α
650   ε
300

ι   540

ξ   148

α IND

ρ   λ

50°

ξ
365

η

IND

ARA

α PAV
Peacock

PAV

60°

40°

TELESCOPIUM

TRIANGULUM

Trianguli Tri The Triangle

Next to Perseus and above the head of Aries lie three faint stars forming an elongated triangle — the constellation Triangulum. Surprisingly enough this constellation dates from antiquity. The Greeks called it Deltoton, the Romans Triangulum and the Arabs Al Muthallath, all meaning 'triangle'. Aratos of Soli described it thus: 'Near Andromeda lies the island of Sicily resembling a triangle whose shorter side is adorned by close-lying stars.' Of interest to us are the three brighter stars of this constellation:

α **Trianguli,** or **Metallah,** is a dwarf star of spectral type F2, in which the hydrogen lines are fainter and the lines of metals more intense. The estimated effective temperature of the star is 7500°K. 64 light years distant, it shines as a star of magnitude 3.58; the absolute magnitude is 2.1.

β **Trianguli** is a dwarf star of spectral type A5, in other words it is a star with a much higher temperature, approximately 10,000°K. Lying at a distance of 230 light years it appears to a terrestrial observer as a star of magnitude 3.08. The absolute brightness is −0.6.

γ **Trianguli** is also a star with a temperature higher than that of the Sun. It is 109 light years distant and the apparent magnitude is 4.07; the absolute magnitude is 1.5.

What the Triangle lacks in number and brightness of stars is compensated for by one single object, the large spiral nebula **M 33** or **NGC 598.** Next to the Andromeda Nebula, it is the largest galaxy in the sky which can be seen with the unaided eye on a clear night, though it is better resolved with prismatic binoculars. It has a very clear nucleus and fewer individual stars; it seems that star clusters and nebular nodes predominate; the spiral arms contain many variable stars. The estimated distance of M 33 is 1,750,000 light years.

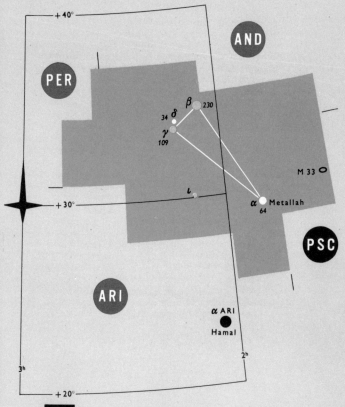

TRI

γ AND
Alamak

AND

PER

β 230

34 δ
γ
109

M 33

ι

α Metallah
64

+40°

+30°

+20°

3h

2h

PSC

ARI

α ARI
Hamal

2
3
4
5

TRIANGULUM

TRIANGULUM AUSTRALE
Trianguli Australis   TrA   The Southern Triangle

Bayer's *Uranometria* shows the Southern Triangle as the counterpart of Triangulum in the northern sky. Whereas the latter is distinguished by its beautiful late-type spiral nebula, Triangulum Australe is represented by three bright stars.

α **Trianguli Australis** is the brightest, for it shines as a star of magnitude 1.88. The spectral type is K5, and the colour is orange, this being directly related to the star's effective surface temperature of 4500°K. The distance from the Earth is 99 light years; the absolute magnitude is −0.5.

β **Trianguli Australis,** 38 light years away, has an apparent magnitude of 3.04. The estimated temperature, corresponding to the spectral class F0 to which it belongs, is 7500°K. The absolute magnitude is an estimated 2.7.

γ **Trianguli Australis.** All that is known of this star is that it has a magnitude of 3.06 and belongs to the group of hydrogen stars which have a surface temperature of about 10,000°K.

δ **Trianguli Australis** might be termed a supplement to the three brighter stars of this constellation. It is somewhat fainter with an apparent magnitude of 4.03 and is a solar type star of spectral group G0. At a distance of 10 parsecs it would be as bright as a star of 1st magnitude. The actual distance from the Earth is 131 light years.

Triangulum Australe contains several variable stars of the cepheid type, but their maximum brightness is a full magnitude below naked eye visibility.

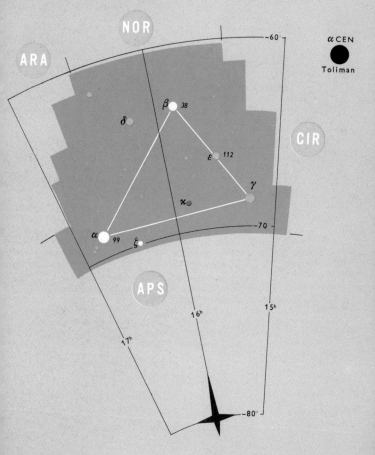

TRIANGULUM AUSTRALE

TUCANA

Tucanae   Tuc   The Toucan

The Toucan, that well-known inhabitant of the zoo, was depicted in the sky by Bayer in his *Uranometria* in 1603. It lies between the constellation Grus and the Small Magellanic Cloud, this galaxy being located south of the chief stars in Tucana.

α **Tucanae** is a star of magnitude 2.91, 142 light years distant from the Earth. The absolute magnitude is -0.3, the spectral type K5, which ranks it among the cooler stars, if one can apply this term to stars with a surface temperature of 4500°K.

$\beta_1\beta_2$ **Tucanae** is a double star of approximately equal magnitudes, 4.52 and 4.48. Both components are of spectral type B9 with an effective surface temperature of about 20,000°K and both are 148 light years distant.

δ **Tucanae,** 220 light years away, shines as a star of magnitude 4.80. It is a helium star, spectral type B9, with an absolute magnitude of 0.7.

47 Tucanae, or **NGC 104,** is a beautiful globular star cluster of the third magnitude occupying a space of 23 minutes. It lies together with the less impressive globular star cluster **NGC 362** in the region of the Small Magellanic Cloud.

The **Small Magellanic Cloud** is an irregular galaxy believed by many astronomers to be a companion of our Galaxy. It and the Large Magellanic Cloud in Dorado are a conglomeration of stars and nebulae and are of asymmetrical shape. Like Polaris, the two are used by sailors to set their course on the seas for they are located close to the south celestial pole.

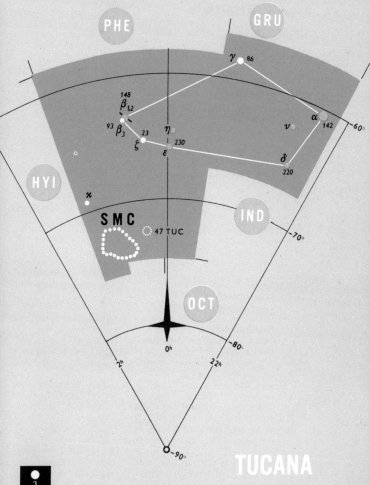

TUC

PHE

GRU

γ 86

148
β₁,₂

93 β₃

23
η

α
142

ν

ζ

ε
230

δ
220

HYI

x

60°

SMC

47 TUC

IND

70°

OCT

0h

80°

2ʰ

22ʰ

90°

TUCANA

3
4
5

URSA MAJOR
Ursae Majoris   UMa   The Great Bear

Through the ages the constellation Ursa Major has been known under various names. It is linked with the nymph Kallisto of Greek mythology. The well-known Plough is only part of the entire constellation.

α **Ursae Majoris,** or **Dubhe,** is the brightest star in UMa. It is a giant of spectral class K0, lying at a distance of 142 light years, and it shines as a star of magnitude 1.95. In reality it is a double star, the two components revolving around a common centre of gravity once every 44 years. It requires a larger telescope to resolve them.

β **Ursae Majoris,** or **Merak,** meaning 'loin', is a giant star, 76 light years distant of spectral type A1, and with an apparent magnitude of 2.44. At 10 parsecs it would be as bright as Capella. The stars Merak, Phekda, Dubhe and Megrez mark the Great Bear's back.

γ **Ursae Majoris,** or **Phekda,** meaning 'thigh', is 80 light years away and shines as a star of magnitude 2.54. The spectral type is A0; the absolute magnitude is 0.6.

δ **Ursae Majoris,** or **Megrez,** 'haunch', is the faintest star in the Plough for, at its distance of 76 light years, it appears to a terrestrial observer as a star of magnitude 3.44. The absolute magnitude is 1.6.

ε **Ursae Majoris,** or **Alioth,** 'tail', is a spectroscopic binary of spectral type A0, 78 light years from the Earth. The apparent magnitude is 1.68, the absolute magnitude 0.2.

η **Ursae Majoris,** or **Benetnash,** is the end star of the Great Bear's tail. It is 163 light years distant, belongs to spectral group B3, and has an apparent magnitude of 1.91. The absolute brightness is −1.6.

ζ **Ursae Majoris,** or **Mizar,** is the most complex star in UMa. In 1889 the spectrum type A2 revealed the presence of another star and later that of a third component. The distance from the Earth is 78 to 80 light years.

80 Ursae Majoris, or **Alcor,** the 'rider', appears to be separated from Mizar by 11.5 minutes of arc (the Moon's diameter is 31 minutes of arc), so that an eye with keen sight is able to resolve the two. In 1908 it was discovered that Alcor itself is also a spectroscopic binary. The distance is 80 light years.

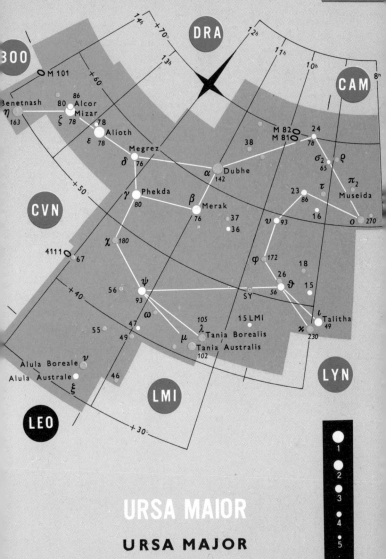

UMA

300

DRA

CAM

M 101

+ 60°

14h

13h

12h

11h

10h

8h

+ 70°

Benetnash
η
163

80 Alcor
ξ 78 Mizar

86

ε 78 Alioth

78

Megrez

δ 76

α Dubhe
142

M 82
M 81

24
78

38

σ₂
65

ρ

π₂

τ

Museida

23
86

16

ο 270

CVN

+ 50°

γ 80 Phekda

β Merak
76

37
36

υ 93

4111 67

χ 180

φ 172

18

26 ϑ
56

15

ψ
93

56

ω

SY

ι Talitha
49

+ 40°

55

47

49

105

λ μ
Tania Borealis

15 LMI

κ
230

46

Alula Boreale ν

Alula Australe ξ

Tania Australis
102

LYN

LMI

LEO

+ 30°

URSA MAIOR

URSA MAJOR

1
2
3
4
5

URSA MINOR
Ursae Minoris   UMi   The Little Bear

α **Ursae Minoris,** or **Polaris,** or **Cynosura,** from the Greek for 'dog's tail', is a giant of spectral class F8 lying at a distance of 470 light years. For centuries it has served to aid sailors to determine their latitude according to its height above the northern horizon. Geographers called it Stella Polaris; for them it was the point marking the Earth's imaginary axis. Polaris is a variable star ranging from magnitude 2.1 to 2.2 in a period of 31.97 days.

β **Ursae Minoris,** or **Kochab,** is a giant star of spectral class K4, 105 light years from the Earth. It has an apparent magnitude of 2.24. At 10 parsecs it would be as bright as Arcturus in Boötes.

γ **Ursae Minoris,** or **Pherkad,** lying at a distance of 180 light years, appears to a terrestrial observer as a star of magnitude 3.14. Its absolute magnitude, however, is such that it would equal Capella in Auriga in brightness at a distance of 10 parsecs. It belongs to spectral class A2.

ε **Ursae Minoris** is a yellow giant of spectral type G1. It is an eclipsing binary with a period of 39.5 days. The slight difference in brightness, only 1/10 stellar magnitude, is not discernible to the naked eye. Its distance from the Earth is 300 light years.

ζ **Ursae Minoris** is a star of spectral type A2 with high surface temperature and apparent magnitude of 4.34 lying at a distance of 220 light years. The absolute magnitude indicates that it is as bright as Arcturus in Boötes.

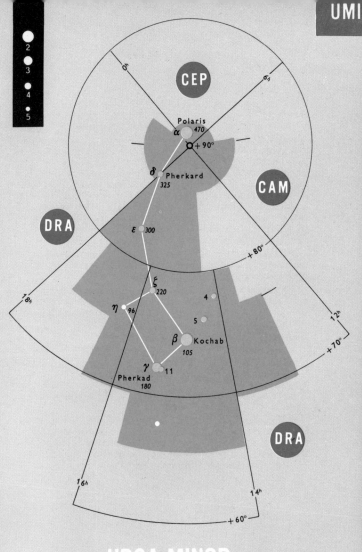

UMI

CEP

CAM

DRA

DRA

Polaris
α 470

+90°

δ Pherkard
325

ε 300

ξ 220

η 96

4

5

β Kochab
105

γ 11
Pherkad
180

+80°

+70°

+60°

0ʰ

6ʰ

12ʰ

14ʰ

16ʰ

18ʰ

2
3
4
5

URSA MINOR

VELA

Velorum   Vel   The Sail

Vela was once part of the constellation Argo Navis. As a result of dividing Argo Navis into three, it happens that Vela has been left with no stars designated α or β.

$\gamma_1\gamma_2$ **Velorum.** At a distance of 650 light years a group of four stars, two of which are seen from Earth as a double star, can be observed even with the smallest telescope. The estimated separation of the double stars is 41 seconds and the brightness of the components is almost equal. They shine as stars of magnitude 2.2, being of spectral type B3 with an estimated temperature about 20,00°K. One of the two other remaining stars of this system has an estimated temperature as high as 50,000°K, the other star is a helium star, with a temperature of 20,000°K.

δ **Velorum,** 63 light years away, shines as a star of magnitude 2.01. The spectrum A0 places it with the so-called hydrogen stars. The absolute magnitude is 0.4.

λ **Velorum,** or **Alsuhail,** is a red super-giant of spectral class K4. The apparent magnitude is 2.22; the distance from the Earth is 820 light years; the absolute magnitude is −5.0.

μ **Velorum** is 105 light years away. The apparent magnitude is 2.84 and the absolute magnitude 0.3. It is a solar type star with a G5 spectrum (the Sun is type G2) and an effective temperature of about 6000°K.

$\varkappa$ **Velorum** is a helium star of spectral type B3, with a temperature of 20,000°K. It is 190 light years distant, and it has an apparent magnitude of 2.63. The absolute magnitude is −1.2.

ψ **Velorum** is a double star of magnitudes 3.64 and 4.2, its components revolving around a common centre in a period of 50 years. It will be at periastron in 1969. The spectral type of both components is that of a dwarf star of class A7. The distance from the Earth is 50 light years.

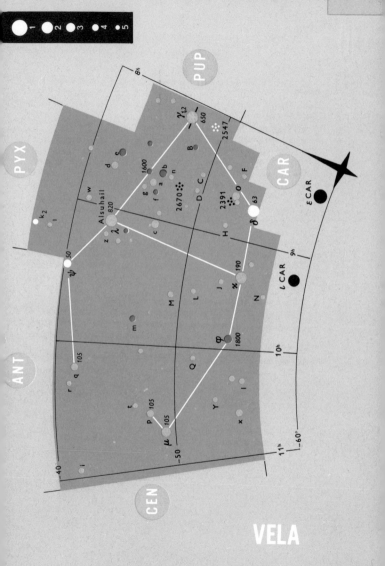

VIRGO
Virginis   Vir   The Virgin

The Sun enters the sixth sign of the zodiac in the autumn solstice. According to mythology Virgo commemorates Astraea, the Greek goddess of justice who lived in the Golden Age.

α **Virginis,** or **Spica,** Latin for 'ear of corn', is the brightest star in this constellation. Lying at a distance of 220 light years, it glows as a star of magnitude 1.21. If it were 10 parsecs distant, it would be much brighter than Sirius. Spica is probably an eclipsing binary. The revolution of the invisible companion is indicated by the shift of lines in the star's spectrum. The period of revolution is 4 days.

β **Virginis, Zavijah,** or **Alaraph.** In Bayer's *Uranometria* this star is in the left wing of Virgo; according to Arab astrologers it marked the place where the Moon had the greatest influence on the happiness of persons born under the sign of Virgo. In reality it is a dwarf sun of spectral class F8, and is of interest because the apparent and absolute magnitudes are identical, viz 3.8, which means that this star is exactly 10 parsecs distant from the Earth.

γ **Virginis,** or **Porrima,** or **Arich.** These are two dwarf suns of spectral type F0, revolving around a common centre of gravity in a period of 172 years. Both have a magnitude of 3.6, and the separation is 5.2 seconds. Light from this star takes only 35 years to reach the Earth.

ε **Virginis,** or **Vindemiatrix,** the feminine of Vindemiator, Latin for 'wine merchant'. Its matutinal (early morning) rising marks the beginning of the vintage. Vindemiatrix is a yellow giant of spectral class G6, lying at a distance of 93 light years.

The constellation Virgo contains a large number of distant galaxies. This clustering comprises some 3000 objects of which 30 are visible with a medium-size telescope.

VIRGO

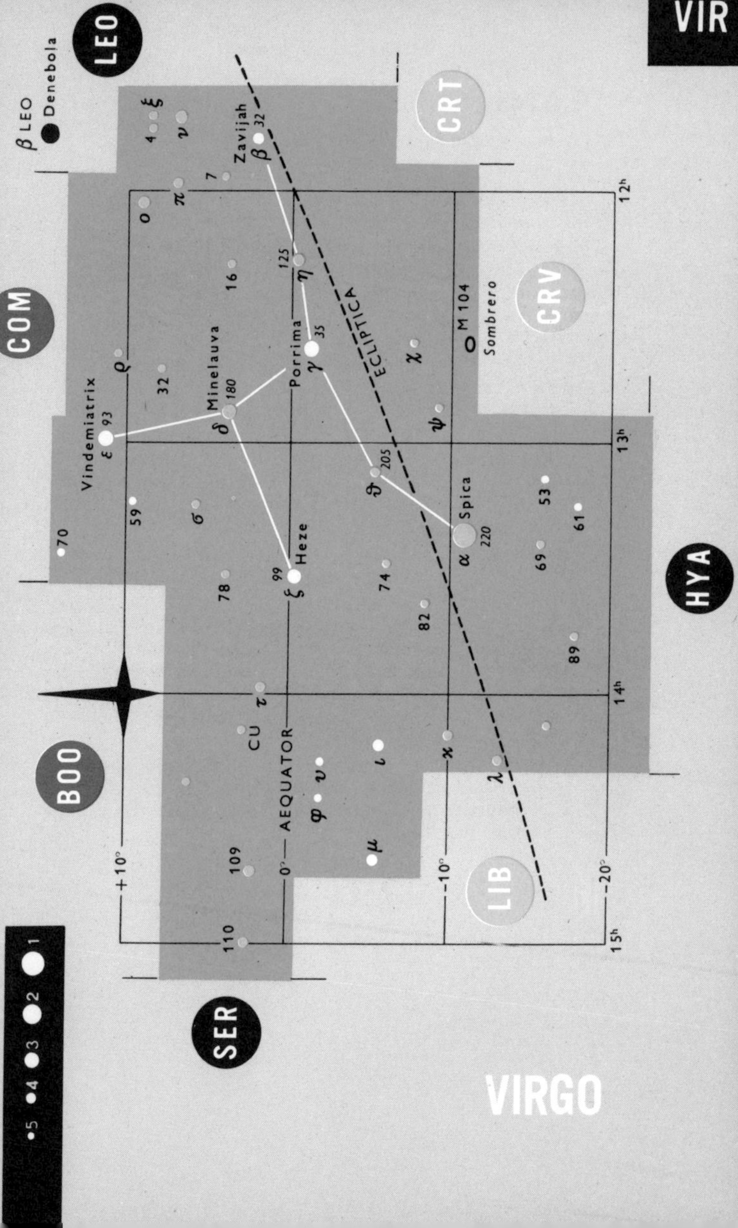
LEO
β LEO
Denebola
CRT
COM
CRV
BOO
HYA
SER
LIB
Zavijah
Vindemiatrix
Minelauva
Porrima
Heze
Spica
M 104
Sombrero
ECLIPTICA
AEQUATOR
12h
13h
14h
15h
+10°
0°
-10°
-20°
CU
•5 •4 ●3 ●2 ●1

VOLANS

Volantis   Vol   The Flying Fish

Bayer's *Uranometria* was the first atlas to include Volans, an abbreviation of the original names Piscis Volans.

α **Volantis** is about 69 light years distant from our Sun, and glows with an apparent magnitude of 4.18. If it were 10 parsecs distant, it would be as bright as α Centauri. The spectrum A5 is that of a white star with a temperature of about 10,000°K.

β **Volantis** is brighter than the foregoing α Vol, having an apparent magnitude of 3.65. The spectral type is K1, characteristic of stars with a temperature lower than that of the Sun. It is 112 light years away.

γ_1 **Volantis** has a brightness of 5.81 at a distance of 130 light years. The spectral type is G0, and the absolute magnitude is 2.8. This star and the following one are an easily resolvable double.

γ_2 **Volantis** has an apparent brightness of 3.87. The spectral type is F5 and the absolute magnitude is 0.9. It lies at a distance of 130 light years.

δ **Volantis** lies farther out in galactic space, and its light takes 1100 years to reach the Earth. The magnitude is 4.02. The spectral type is F5, wherein the lines of metals are most intense and absorption bands produced by molecules begin to appear. At a distance of 10 parsecs δ Volantis would be as bright as the planet Venus.

ξ **Volantis** is a star of magnitude 3.89, 116 light years distant. Its spectrum places it in the group of K0 stars with a surface temperature lower than that of the Sun. The absolute magnitude is 1.1.

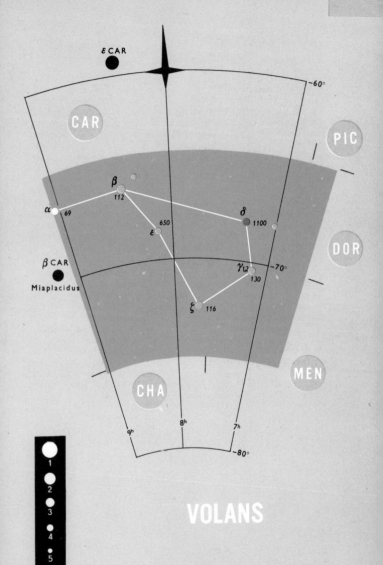

VOL

VOLANS

VULPECULA
Vulpeculae   Vul   The Fox

Hevelius, mayor of Danzig, was a very good astronomer, designer and maker of measuring instruments besides being an excellent graphic artist, but he tended to crowd the sky with unnecessary constellations. He designated a region in the heavens which had always been part of Cygnus as Vulpecula sum Ansere, meaning 'the little fox with the goose'. Modern astronomy removed the goose but the International Astronomical Union decided that the constellation the Little Fox should remain. From the stellar viewpoint this constellation is of minor importance and this atlas deals with only the one star below.

α **Vulpeculae** shines as a star of magnitude 4.63; its light takes 270 years to reach the Earth. It is a red giant of spectral group M1, with an estimated temperature of 3500°K. The absolute magnitude is 0.0.

Of far greater significance in this constellation is the large planetary nebula **M 27** or **NGC 6853** called **Dumb-bell.** The apparent dimensions are 480 seconds by 240 seconds. The stellar magnitude is 7.6 and the distance 150 parsecs. A medium-sized telescope is required for resolution. Photographs made with different exposure times show the extent of the gaseous shell which is still expanding. The fantastic velocity condemns planetary nebulae to a relatively short lifetime. Unlike diffuse gaseous nebulae which derive their luminosity from adjacent hot stars, planetary nebulae are glowing objects distinguished by the expansion of the shell of exceptionally high temperature material surrounding a central star of nucleus.

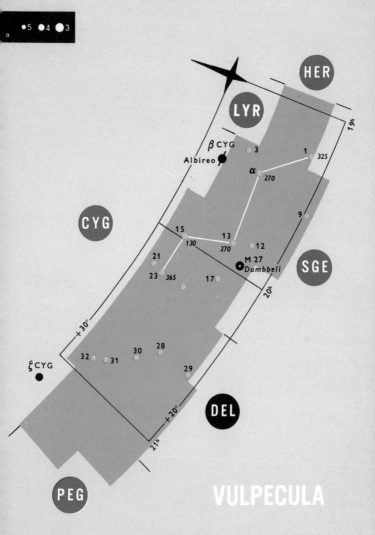

VUL

•5 •4 ●3

HER

LYR

β CYG
Albireo

3

1   325

α
270

CYG

9

15   13
130   270

12

M 27
Dumbbell

SGE

21

23   365

17

+30°

20ʰ

28

32   31   30

29

ξ CYG

+20°

DEL

21ʰ

PEG

VULPECULA

Glossary

ALMUCANTAR
Circle of constant altitude above the horizon.

ALTITUDE
Angle of elevation of a star above the horizon. It is expressed in degrees: positive ($+$) if the star is above the horizon and negative ($-$) if it is below the horizon.

ANGULAR MEASURE
The magnitude of an angle expressed in degrees. A circle is divided into 360° (degrees), each degree into 60′ (minutes of arc), and each minute into 60″ (seconds of arc). The correlation between the measurement of an angle in degrees and in terms of time units (caused by the Earth's rotation) is as follows:

$$1° \; - \; 4 \text{ m}$$
$$1′ \; - \; 4 \text{ s}$$
$$1″ \; - \; 1/15 \text{ s} \quad \text{See } \textit{Angular Measure, Time.}$$

ANGULAR MEASURE, TIME
The size of an angle expressed in time units — commonly used in astronomy. The relation between time units and degrees is based on the following: the Earth makes one complete revolution of 360° in 24 hours. One hour, therefore, represents a rotation of 15°. One hour consists of 60 minutes and one minute of 60 seconds. 1h $= 60$ m $= 3600$ s, 1 h $= 15°$, 1 m $= 15′$, 1 s $= 15″$. For the inverse relationship, see *Angular Measure*.

APPULSE
As the Moon moves across the sky, it eclipses the stars in its path. Such an eclipse is called an occultation and is visible only from certain parts of the Earth. At some places the Moon will make only a very close approach, which is termed an appulse.

ASTROPHYSICS
A branch of astronomy dealing with the physical and chemical constitution of the celestial bodies and of the physical phenomena occurring therein.

ATOM, EXCITED
An atom in which one of the electrons has jumped to a higher energy level under the influence of incoming energy (radiation, collision, etc.). The return to the original level results in the radiation of photons.

AZIMUTH
Angle (with apex at the zenith) formed by the star's vertical circle with the meridian. It is usually measured in degrees from the south point westwards. It is one of the horizontal coordinates.

BRIGHTNESS, STELLAR
Apparent stellar magnitude. First it is necessary to elucidate the terms *luminosity* and *intensity of radiation*. Stars were classed according to brightness, or apparent magnitude, as long as 2000 years ago, the brightest being classed as stars of the first magnitude, the faintest ones still visible with the unaided eye as stars of the 6th magnitude. At the present day this term has been more precisely defined. Let us take two stars differing in brightness by five magnitudes. To the observer, the ratio of their intensity of radiation is 1 : 100; in other words, one magnitude is equal to the fifth root of 100, i.e. 2.512. Thus a star of the 3rd magnitude is 2.512 times as bright as one of the 4th magnitude. The apparent stellar magnitude thus permits a certain classification of the star's brightness as it appears to the terrestrial observer. It tells us nothing about the star's actual luminosity nor about its diameter. The true luminosity of a star is related to the *absolute stellar magnitude*, which can be deduced, if we know the apparent stellar magnitude and the star's distance from the Earth, according to this formula:
$M = m + 5 + 5 \log d$, where M is the absolute stellar magnitude, m the apparent stellar magnitude, and d the star's parallax in parsecs.

CHROMOSPHERE
The layer of the Sun's or a star's atmosphere between the photosphere and the corona.

CIRCUMPOLAR CONSTELLATIONS
Constellations which, viewed from a given point on the Earth's surface, never go below the horizon. At the North

and South Poles, all stars are circumpolar; at the equator none.

COLURE, VERNAL EQUINOCTIAL
The hour circle passing through the vernal equinox.

COORDINATE SYSTEMS

Reference planes and directions	Starting point	Coordinates
Horizon and local meridian	South point	Azimuth A Altitude h
Celestial equator and local meridian	Point of intersection	Declination δ Hour angle t
Celestial equator and vernal equinox	Vernal point	Declination δ Right ascension α
Geographical — Terrestrial equator and Greenwich meridian	Point of intersection	Geographical latitude φ Geographical longitude λ

There are also other coordinate systems such as the ecliptic, galactic, etc.

CORONA
The outermost layer of the Sun's atmosphere, reaching far out into interplanetary space and appearing as a grey halo around the Moon's dark disc during a total eclipse of the Sun.

CULMINATION
The instant when a celestial body crosses the meridian: either upper culmination (maximum altitude) or lower culmination (minimum altitude).

DECLINATION
The angular distance of a body from the celestial equator. It is measured in degrees positive (+) for angles north of the equator and degrees negative (−) for angles south of the equator. Declination is denoted by the small Greek letter delta (δ).

DWARF
A star the same size or smaller than the Sun, of spectral type F, G, K, M, or one belonging to the group of so-called white dwarfs — stars of great density and minimum diameter.

ECLIPTIC
The path of the Earth's orbit around the Sun.

ELECTRON
An elementary particle of matter. Its mass is 1/1840 that of a proton, i.e. 9.1×10^{-28} grams. The negative charge equals -4.8×10^{-10} E.S.U. The electron is bound to a definite orbit around the nucleus of an atom. When under the influence of an external force it passes suddenly into another orbit, the atom absorbs or emits a definite quantum of energy in the form of a light quantum — a photon.

EPHEMERIS
Forecast of the positions and motions of the celestial bodies, generally issued for the whole year at the beginning of each civil year.

EQUATOR, CELESTIAL
The great circle of the celestial sphere whose plane is perpendicular to the axis of the Earth. It divides the sky into the northern and southern hemispheres.

EQUATOR, TERRESTRIAL
A great circle of the Earth that is everywhere equidistant from the two poles and divides the Earth's surface into the northern and southern hemispheres.

FORCE
A physical quantity. An agency or influence that if applied to a free body results in acceleration of that body; also the ability of a body to act or produce an effect (work) in the physical sense.
Force = mass × acceleration. Work = force × distance.
Force may be gravitational, nuclear, magnetic, etc.

GALAXY
A stellar system shaped like a circular band and comprising some 100 to 150 billion stars, nebulae and star clusters. The

Sun is one of the stars of such a galaxy. The diameter of our Galaxy, called the Milky Way, is 100,000 light years. The Universe contains many other galaxies recorded in the literature of astronomy as spiral nebulae or extragalactic nebulae. For details see page 27 of text.

GIANT
A star larger than the Sun. Such a star may be a sub-giant, giant or super-giant.

GREEK ALPHABET:

α, A	alpha	ι, I	iota	ϱ, P	rho
β, B	beta	$\varkappa, K$	kappa	σ, Σ	sigma
γ, Γ	gamma	λ, Λ	lambda	τ, T	tau
δ, Δ	delta	μ, M	mu	υ, Y	upsilon
ε, E	epsilon	ν, N	nu	φ, Φ	phi
ζ, Z	zeta	ξ, Ξ	xi	χ, X	chi
η, H	eta	o, O	omicron	ψ, Ψ	psi
$\vartheta, \theta, \Theta$	theta	π, Π	pi	ω, Ω	omega

HELIACAL RISING
The first rising of a star after its period of invisibility due to conjunction with the Sun. On its apparent journey among the stars throughout the year the Sun outshines, for a time, the brightness of nearby stars thus making them invisible. For example, Orion is not visible in late June because it is directly beneath the sun in Gemini at the time.

HELIACAL SETTING
The last setting of a star before its period of invisibility.

HOUR ANGLE
The angle between the celestial meridian of an observer and the hour circle of a celestial object measured westward from the meridian. It is measured in hours from 0 to 24. See *Coordinate Systems*.

INTENSITY OF RADIATION
The quantity of radiant energy passing per unit time through a unit surface placed perpendicular to the direction of the electromagnetic waves.

ION
An atom that carries a positive or negative electric charge as

a result of having gained or lost one or more electrons.
A non-ionized atom is electrically neutral.

LATITUDE, GEOGRAPHICAL
The angular distance north or south of the Earth's equator
measured through 90 degrees and expressed in positive ($+$)
degrees north of the equator and negative ($-$) degrees
south of the equator.

LONGITUDE, GEOGRAPHICAL
The angular distance between the meridian of a given place
and the prime (Greenwich) meridian. It is expressed in
degrees east and west of Greenwich.

LIGHT
An electromagnetic radiation to which the eye is sensitive
and which travels in a vacuum in a straight line from the
source with a speed of about 300,000 kilometres per second
(186,000 miles per second).

LIGHT YEAR
The distance that light travels is one year in a vacuum,
which equals 9.46×10^{12} kilometres or approximately
10,000,000,000,000 km. (6 million million miles).

LUMINOUS INTENSITY
In physics: the luminous flux emitted by a source in a unit
solid angle.
In stars: the total energy radiated from a star's surface in
one second.

LUX
A unit of illumination equal to the direct illumination on
a surface from a point source of a luminosity of one standard
candle located at a distance of one metre.

MAGNITUDE, ABSOLUTE STELLAR
The brightness (magnitude) of a star at the distance of
10 parsecs. In other words it does not denote the diameter
of the star but its luminosity. If we designate the absolute
stellar magnitude with the letter M, then $M = m + 5 +
+ 5 \log d$, where m is the apparent magnitude and d the
star's parallax in parsecs.

MAGNITUDE, APPARENT STELLAR
See *Brightness*.

MERIDIAN, TERRESTRIAL (PRINCIPAL OR STANDARD)
The great circle passing through an agreed point of reference on the Earth's surface (Greenwich) and through the poles.

MERIDIAN, CELESTIAL
The great circle of the celestial sphere passing through the celestial poles and the zenith and nadir of a given place. See *Coordinate Systems*.

MERIDIAN, LOCAL
The meridian passing through the position of the observer on the Earth's surface.

MERIDIAN LINE
The line joining the north and south points, tangent to the meridian passing through the point of the observer.

NOVA
A star temporarily increasing in brightness by 10 to 16 stellar magnitudes in a few days as a result of the sudden explosive expansion of its gaseous shell. As a rule, within several days it fades by several magnitudes and regains its original magnitude after several years.

PARALLAX
Angle subtended at a distant object by the baseline. In astronomy, it is taken to mean the angle subtended at the star by half the baseline, i.e. by the radius of the Earth or of its orbit. Stellar parallax is expressed in seconds of arc.

PARALLAX, TRIGONOMETRIC
The angle of parallax is measured according to the displacement of a star against the distant stellar background. This change in position is caused by the annual motion of the Earth around the Sun. Stellar distances can be determined trigonometrically from the triangle formed by the star, Sun and Earth.

271

PARSEC
A unit for expressing stellar distance. It corresponds to the distance from which the mean distance of the Earth from Sun would appear as a parallax of 1 second of arc. The mean distance of the Earth from the Sun, termed an astronomical unit (AU) is 149,600,000 kilometres. One parsec equals 3.26 light years.

PHOTON
A quantum of radiant energy produced, for example, by the passage of an electron from a higher to a lower energy level in an atom. The energy of the emitted photon depends on the type of atom and on which levels in the atom were affected by the passage. The wavelength of the resulting radiation is inversely proportional to the energy of the photons producing the radiation. The photon is the only source of information on the very distant phenomena of the universe, retaining this information throughout its entire journey through space, sometimes taking millions of years. See also *Spectrum*.

PHOTOSPHERE
The visible luminous surface of the Sun or a star.

PLANET
A spherical celestial body shining by reflected light and revolving around a central star. The Earth is a planet revolving around the Sun, as are Mercury, Venus, Mars, Jupiter, Saturn, Uranus, Neptune and Pluto.

POLES, CELESTIAL
Points of intersection of the celestial axis (also the Earth's axis) and the celestial sphere.

POLES, TERRESTRIAL
Points of intersection of the Earth's surface and Earth's axis. Either extremity of the Earth's axis.

PRECESSION
A comparatively slow gyration of the rotation of a spinning body about another line intersecting it so as to describe a cone. It is caused by the application of a torque tending to change the direction of the axis of rotation. This is true also

of the Earth's rotation, the celestial poles describing an elliptical path in the heavens in a period of 26,000 years. In consequence of the Earth's precession, the vernal equinox moves westward along the ecliptic and so do the signs of the zodiac in relation to the constellations. See page 62, Fig. 17.

REFLECTOR
A telescope in which the principal focusing element is a mirror.

REFRACTOR
A telescope in which the principal focusing element is usually an achromatic lens.

RIGHT ASCENSION (RA)
Angle, measured eastward, from the vernal equinox in the plane of the equator to the star's hour circle. See *Coordinate Systems*.

SIDEREAL TIME
The hour angle of the vernal equinox. Because of the Earth's rotation, the sky appears to make a complete revolution of 360° in 24 hours sidereal time. When the vernal equinox passes through the meridian, it is zero hour sidereal time. Sidereal time is equal to the sum of a star's right ascension and its hour angle; in other words the right ascension of stars passing through the meridian gives us the sidereal time. Sidereal time, then, informs us which constellations are on the meridian at a given moment and thus of the position of the whole celestial sphere.

SPECTRAL TYPE
The classification of stars based on an analysis of their *spectra*.

SPECTRUM
Light from a source (e.g. starlight) dispersed according to colour or wavelength by means of a prism or other device, e.g. a diffraction grating. The rainbow, for example, is a spectrum caused by the dispersion of sunlight through drops of water. The following terms will elucidate the matter further.

EMISSION SPECTRUM
Bright lines or bands on a dark ground produced by an incandescent source.

ABSORPTION SPECTRUM
Dark lines or bands on a light ground produced by the presence of cooler or cold matter between the observer and the incandescent source. The elements contained therein emit light of less intensity and therefore the respective lines are dark.

LINE SPECTRUM
The arrangement of lines characteristic of each element.

BAND SPECTRUM
Vertical bands, which detailed analysis proves to be composed of closely grouped single lines. This spectrum indicates the molecules of elements and compounds.

CONTINUOUS SPECTRUM
A continuous band of varying colours arranged in the following order: violet, indigo, blue, green, yellow, orange, red. Detailed analysis reveals that it is composed of a system of lines and bands. The star's sub-surface layer emits light which produces a continuous spectrum by dispersion. The atmosphere of a cooler star is revealed by a system of absorption lines. The spectrum makes it possible to determine the composition of a star's atmosphere, its temperature, velocity of rotation, velocity of recession or of approach, whether it is a double star, etc.

SPECTROSCOPIC BINARY
A pair of stars which cannot be resolved with a telescope. A doubling of the spectral lines, however, reveals the presence of a second component.

STAR
A celestial body, usually spheroidal, which is self-luminous as a result of nuclear processes in the stellar interior. The Sun is a star. Because of their great distance from the Earth, other stars are seen only as pinpoints of light though their diameter and luminiscence may be far greater than that of the Sun.

STELLAR CHARACTERISTIC
A quantity denoting some property of a star, namely position, distance, apparent and absolute magnitudes, temperature (colour), mass, diameter.

SUPERNOVA
A nova of astounding brilliance whose increase in brightness is several magnitudes greater than that of a normal nova. The fundamental characteristics of this phenomenon are different from those of a normal nova. Most probably it is a case of a rapid and large-scale nuclear reaction in the interior of a star.

THERMOMETRIC SCALE
A scale for measuring temperature established by designating certain temperature levels (e.g. the boiling point and freezing point of substances) with a given number, and so fixing the size of the intervals (degrees) and the beginning and end of the scale.

	Centigrade	Reaumur	Fahrenheit	Kelvin
Freezing point of water	0°C	0°R	32°F	273.16°K
Boiling point of water	100°C	80°R	212°F	373.16°K

VARIABLE STAR
A star whose brightness varies. The cause of such variation may be either geometric (temporary eclipsing by another star circling about it in a regular orbit) or physical (as a result of changes in the condition of the star's outer layers).

VERNAL EQUINOX
One of the two points on the celestial sphere where the celestial equator intersects the ecliptic. The Sun is at the vernal equinox when day and night in spring are of equal length (about March 21).

VERTICAL CIRCLES
Great circles of the celestial sphere passing through the zenith and nadir. They are perpendicular to the horizon.

ZENITH
The highest point in the heavens directly above the observer

as determined by the infinite upward extension of a plumb line.

ZODIAC

The zone along the ecliptic denoting the apparent path of the Sun throughout the year and passing through the following constellations: Aries, Taurus, Gemini, Cancer, Leo, Virgo, Libra, Scorpius, Sagittarius, Capricornus, Aquarius, Pisces.

ALPHABETICAL LIST OF STARS
found in the Text and on the Maps

Name of Star	Designation		Page	Right Ascension h m		Declination ° '	
Acamar	ϑ	Eri	158	02	56	−40	30
Achernar	α	Eri	158	01	36	−57	29
Achird	η	Cas	124	00	46	+57	33
Acrab	β	Sco	232	16	03	−19	40
Acrux	α	Cru	146	12	23	−62	49
Acubens	α	Cnc	112	08	56	+12	03
Adara	ε	CMa	116	06	57	−28	54
Adhafera	ζ	Leo	178	10	14	+23	40
Agena	β	Cen	126	14	00	−60	08
Ain	ε	Tau	242	04	26	+19	04
Alamak	γ	And	90	02	01	+42	05
Alaraph	β	Vir	258	11	48	+02	03
Albali	ε	Aqr	96	20	45	−09	41
Albireo	β	Cyg	148	19	29	+27	51
Alchita (Al Chiba)	α	Crv	144	12	06	−24	27
Alcor	80	UMa	252	13	23	+55	15
Alcyone	η	Tau	242	03	45	+23	57
Aldebaran	α	Tau	242	04	33	+16	25
Alderamin	α	Cep	128	21	17	+62	22
Alfard	α	Hya	170	09	25	−08	26
Algenib	γ	Peg	210	00	11	+14	54
Algenib	α	Per	212	03	21	+49	41
Algieba	γ	Leo	178	10	17	+20	06
Algol	β	Per	212	03	05	+40	46
Algorab	δ	Crv	144	12	27	−16	14
Alhena	γ	Gem	162	06	53	+16	27
Alioth	ε	UMa	252	12	52	+56	14
Alkalurops	μ	Boo	106	15	23	+37	33
Alkes	α	Crt	144	10	57	−18	02
Alnair	α	Gru	164	22	05	−47	12
Alnilam	ε	Ori	206	05	34	−01	14
Alnitak	ζ	Ori	206	05	38	−01	58
Alphirk (Alfirk)	β	Cep	128	21	28	+70	20
Alrai (Arrai)	γ	Cep	128	23	37	−77	21

Name of Star	Designation		Page	Right Ascension h m		Declination ° '	
Alrami	α	Sgr	230	19	20	−40	43
Alrisha (Al Rischa)	α	Psc	218	01	59	+02	31
Alshain	β	Aql	98	19	53	+06	17
Alsuhail	λ	Vel	256	09	06	−43	14
Altair	α	Aql	98	19	48	+08	44
Aludra	η	CMa	116	07	22	−29	12
Alula Australe	ξ	UMa	252	11	16	+31	49
Alula Boreale	ν	UMa	252	11	16	+33	22
Alwaid	β	Dra	154	17	29	+52	20
Alya	ϑ	Ser	238	18	54	+04	08
Ancha	ζ	Aqr	96	22	14	−08	02
Antares	α	Sco	232	16	26	−26	19
Arcturus	α	Boo	106	14	13	+19	27
Arich	γ	Vir	258	12	39	−01	11
Arkab Prior	β₁	Sgr	230	19	19	−44	33
Arkab Posterior	β₂	Sgr	230	19	20	−44	54
Arneb	α	Lep	182	05	31	−17	51
Ascella	ζ	Sgr	230	18	59	−29	57
Ascellus Australis	δ	Cnc	112	08	42	+18	20
Ascellus Borealis	γ	Cnc	112	08	40	+21	39
Asterion	β	CVn	114	12	31	+41	38
Asterope	21	Tau	242	03	43	+24	24
Atiks	o	Per	212	03	41	+32	08
Atlas	27	Tau	242	03	46	+23	54
Azelfafage	π₁	Cyg	148	21	40	+50	58
Azmidiske	ξ	Pup	222	07	47	−04	44
Baten Kaitos	ζ	Cet	130	01	49	−10	35
Beid	o₁	Eri	158	04	09	−06	58
Bellatrix	γ	Ori	206	05	22	+06	18
Benetnash	η	UMa	252	13	46	+49	34
Betelgeuse	α	Ori	206	05	52	+07	24
Botein	δ	Ari	102	03	09	+19	32
Canopus	α	Car	122	06	21	−52	40
Capella	α	Aur	104	05	13	+45	57
Caph	β	Cas	124	00	06	+58	52
Castor	α	Gem	162	07	31	+32	00
Celaeno	16	Tau	242	03	42	+24	08

Name of Star	Designation		Page	Right Ascension h m		Declination ° ′	
Cih	γ	Cas	124	00	53	+60	26
Cor Caroli	α	CVn	114	12	54	+38	35
Coxa	ϑ	Leo	178	11	12	+15	42
Cursa	β	Eri	158	05	05	−05	09
Dabih	β	Cap	120	20	18	−14	56
Deneb Cygni	α	Cyg	148	20	40	+45	06
Deneb Algiedi	δ	Cap	120	21	44	−16	21
Deneb Kaitos	β	Cet	130	00	41	−18	16
Deneb Okab	δ	Aql	98	19	23	+03	35
Denebola	β	Leo	178	11	47	+14	51
Diadem	α	Com	138	13	08	+17	48
Dschubba	δ	Sco	232	15	57	−22	29
Dubhe	α	UMa	252	11	01	+62	01
Electra	17	Tau	242	03	42	+23	57
Enif	ε	Peg	210	21	42	+09	39
Etamin	γ	Dra	154	17	55	+51	30
Fomalhaut	α	PsA	220	22	55	−29	53
Furud	ζ	CMa	116	06	18	−30	02
Gemma	α	CrB	142	15	33	+26	53
Gienah	ε	Cyg	148	20	44	+33	47
Gomeisa	β	CMi	118	07	24	+08	23
Grafias	ζ	Sco	232	16	51	−42	17
Gredi	α	Cap	120	20	15	−12	42
Hamal	α	Ari	102	02	04	+23	14
Haris	γ	Boo	106	14	30	+38	32
Hassaleh	ι	Aur	104	04	54	+33	05
Hatysa	ι	Ori	206	05	33	−05	56
Heka	λ	Ori	206	05	32	+09	54
Heze	ζ	Vir	258	13	32	−00	20
Homam	ζ	Peg	210	22	39	+10	34
Izar	ε	Boo	106	14	43	+27	17
Kaffaljidhma	γ	Cet	130	02	41	+03	02
Kajam	ω	Her	166	16	23	+14	09
Kaus Australis	ε	Sgr	230	18	21	−34	25
Kaus Borealis	λ	Sgr	230	18	25	−25	27
Kaus Medius (Kaus Meridionalis)	δ	Sgr	230	18	18	−29	51
Kelb Alrai (Cebalrai)	β	Oph	204	17	41	+04	35

Name of Star	Designation		Page	Right Ascension		Declination	
				h	m	°	'
Kerb	τ	Peg	210	23	18	+23	28
Kochab	β	UMi	254	14	51	+74	22
Kraz	β	Crv	144	12	32	−23	07
Ksora (Ruckbar)	δ	Cas	124	01	23	+59	59
Kuma	ν	Dra	154	17	31	+55	13
Lesath	ν	Sco	232	16	09	−19	20
Maasym	λ	Her	166	17	29	+26	09
Maia	20	Tau	242	03	43	+24	13
Markab	α	Peg	210	23	02	+14	56
Matar	η	Peg	210	22	41	+29	58
Mebsuta	ε	Gem	162	06	41	+25	11
Megrez	δ	UMa	252	12	13	+57	19
Menkalinan	β	Aur	104	05	56	+44	57
Menkar	α	Cet	130	03	00	+03	54
Menkhib	ζ	Per	212	03	51	+31	44
Merak	β	UMa	252	10	59	+56	39
Merope	23	Tau	242	03	43	+23	48
Mesarthim	γ	Ari	102	01	51	+19	03
Metallah	α	Tri	246	01	50	+29	20
Miaplacidus	β	Car	122	09	13	−69	31
Minelauva	δ	Vir	258	12	53	+03	40
Minkar	ε	Crv	144	12	08	−22	20
Mintaka	δ	Ori	206	05	29	−00	20
Mira	o	Cet	130	02	17	−03	12
Mirach	β	And	90	01	07	+35	21
Mirfak	α	Per	212	03	21	+49	41
Mirzam	β	CMa	116	06	20	−17	56
Misam	κ	Per	212	03	06	+44	40
Mizar	ζ	UMa	252	13	22	+55	11
Muliphein	γ	CMa	116	07	01	−15	33
Museida	π_2	UMa	252	08	36	+64	30
Naos	ζ	Pup	222	08	02	−39	52
Nash	γ	Sgr	230	18	03	−30	26
Nashira	γ	Cap	120	21	37	−16	53
Nath	β	Tau	242	05	23	+28	34
Nekkar	β	Boo	106	15	00	+40	35
Nihal	β	Lep	182	05	26	−20	48
Nodus I	ζ	Dra	154	17	09	+65	47
Nodus II	δ	Dra	154	19	13	+67	34

Name of Star	Designation		Page	Right Ascension		Declination	
				h	m	°	'
Nunki	σ	Sgr	230	19	01	−21	49
Peacock	α	Pav	208	20	21	−56	53
Phakt	α	Col	136	05	38	−34	06
Phekda	γ	UMa	252	11	51	+53	58
Pherkad	γ	UMi	254	15	21	+72	01
Pherkard	δ	UMi	254	17	48	+86	37
Pleione	BU	Tau	242	03	46	+23	59
Polaris	α	UMi	254	01	49	+89	02
Pollux	β	Gem	162	07	42	+28	09
Porrima	γ	Vir	254	12	39	−01	11
Procyon	α	CMi	118	07	37	+05	21
Pulcherrima	ε	Boo	106	14	43	+27	17
Rana	δ	Eri	158	03	41	−09	56
Ras Algethi	α	Her	166	17	12	+14	27
Ras Alhague	α	Oph	204	17	33	+12	36
Ras Elased Austr.	ε	Leo	178	09	43	+24	00
Ras Elased Bor.	μ	Leo	178	09	50	+26	15
Reda (Tarazed)	γ	Aql	98	19	44	+10	29
Regulus	α	Leo	178	10	06	+12	13
Rigel	β	Ori	206	05	12	−08	15
Rotanev	β	Del	150	20	35	+14	25
Rutilicus	β	Her	166	16	04	+21	35
Sabik	η	Oph	204	17	08	−15	40
Sadalachbia (Sadachbia)	γ	Aqr	96	22	19	−01	38
Sadalmelek	α	Aqr	96	22	03	−00	34
Sadalsud	β	Aqr	96	21	29	−05	48
Sadir	γ	Cyg	148	20	20	+40	06
Saiph	κ	Ori	206	05	45	−09	41
Sarin	δ	Her	166	17	13	+24	54
Scheat	β	Peg	210	23	01	+27	49
Schedir (Schedar)	α	Cas	124	00	38	+56	16
Segin	ε	Cas	124	01	51	+63	25
Sham	α	Sge	228	19	38	+17	54
Shaula	λ	Sco	232	17	30	−37	04
Sheliak	β	Lyr	190	18	48	+33	18
Sheratan	β	Ari	102	01	52	+20	34
Sirius	α	CMa	116	06	43	−16	39

Name of Star	Designation		Page	Right Ascension		Declination	
				h	m	°	′
Sirrah	α	And	90	00	06	+28	49
Skat	δ	Aqr	96	22	52	−16	05
Spica	α	Vir	258	13	23	−10	54
Sulaphat	γ	Lyr	190	18	57	+32	37
Svalocin (Sualocin)	α	Del	150	20	37	+15	44
Talitha	ι	UMa	252	08	56	+48	14
Tania Australis	μ	UMa	252	10	19	+41	45
Tania Borealis	λ	UMa	252	10	14	+43	10
Taygeta	19	Tau	242	03	42	+24	19
Tejat Prior	η	Gem	162	06	12	+22	31
Tejat Posterior	μ	Gem	162	06	20	+22	32
Theemin	v₂	Eri	158	04	34	−30	40
Thuban	α	Dra	154	14	03	+64	37
Toliman	α	Cen	126	14	36	−60	38
Tureis	ι	Car	122	09	15	−59	03
Unuk Elhaia (Unuk al hay)	α	Ser	238	15	42	+06	35
Vega	α	Lyr	190	18	35	+38	44
Vindemiatrix	ε	Vir	258	13	00	+11	14
Wasat	δ	Gem	162	07	17	+22	05
Wezen	δ	CMa	116	07	06	−26	19
Yed Prior	δ	Oph	204	16	12	−03	34
Yed Posterior	ε	Oph	204	16	16	−04	34
Zaurak	γ	Eri	158	03	56	−13	39
Zavijah (Zavijava)	β	Vir	258	11	48	+02	03
Zibal	ζ	Eri	158	03	13	−09	00
Zosma	δ	Leo	178	11	11	+20	48
Zuben Elakrab	γ	Lib	184	15	33	−14	37
Zuben Elakribi	δ	Lib	184	14	58	−08	19
Zuben Elgenubi	α	Lib	184	14	48	−15	50
Zuben Elschemali	β	Lib	184	15	14	−09	12
Zuben Hakrabi	ν	Lib	184	15	04	−16	04

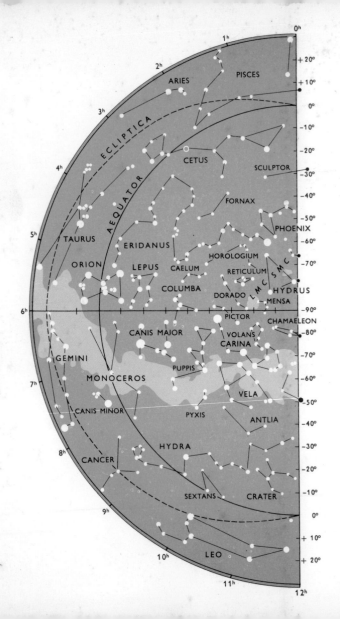